METHODICAL ANALYSIS OF EDUCATION

METHODICAL ANALYSIS OF EDUCATION

B.A., B.Ed., M.A., M.Ed. M.Phil & Research Courses for Indian Universities

GUPTAJIT PATHAK

M.A. (History, Political Science, Sociology), B.Ed., M.Phil.
Research Scholar, Member of N.C.E.R.T. and I.H.C.
&
Ex. Lecturer, Deptt. of History, P.B. Anchalik College, Barenghati, Kamrup
Under Gauhati University, Guwahati, Assam
Ex. Head, Faculty of Social Sciences, Donyi-Polo Vidya Bhawan,
Itanagar, Aruncahal Pradesh
Presently Principal, Arunachal Community College & Health Sciences
Under Rajiv Gandhi University, Itanagar, Arunachal Pradesh
&
Visiting Faculty, Magnanimous Endeavours Group (MEG)
An NGO for UPSC and APPSC Coaching
Itanagar, Arunachal Pradesh

PUBLISHING FOR ONE WORLD

NEW AGE INTERNATIONAL (P) LIMITED, PUBLISHERS

New Delhi • Bangalore • Chennai • Cochin • Guwahati • Hyderabad
Jalandhar • Kolkata • Lucknow • Mumbai • Ranchi
Visit us at **www.newagepublishers.com**

Published by New Age International (P) Ltd., Publishers
First Edition: 2010

Branches:
- 36, Malikarjuna Temple Street, Opp. ICWA, Basavanagudi, **Bangalore**. ✆ (080) 26677815
- 26, Damodaran Street, T. Nagar, **Chennai**. ✆ (044) 24353401
- CE-39/1016, Carrier Station Road, Near Paulson Park Hotel, Ernakulam South, **Cochin.** ✆ (0484) 4051303
- Hemsen Complex, Mohd. Shah Road, Paltan Bazar, Near Starline Hotel, **Guwahati**. ✆ (0361) 2543669
- No. 105, 1st Floor, Madhiray Kaveri Tower, 3-2-19, Azam Jahi Road, Nimboliadda, **Hyderabad**. ✆ (040) 24652456
- RDB Chambers (Formerly Lotus Cinema) 106A,1st Floor, S.N. Banerjee Road, **Kolkata**. ✆ (033) 22275247
- 16-A, Jopling Road, **Lucknow**. ✆ (0522) 2209578
- 142C, Victor House, Ground Floor, N.M. Joshi Marg, Lower Parel, **Mumbai**. ✆ (022) 24927869
- 22, Golden House, Daryaganj, **New Delhi**. ✆ (011) 23262370, 23262368

ISBN : 978-81-224-2784-4

Rs. 100.00

C-09-08-4059

Printed in India at Ajit Printers, Delhi.
Typeset by author

PUBLISHING FOR ONE WORLD
NEW AGE INTERNATIONAL (P) LIMITED, PUBLISHERS
4835/24, Ansari Road, Daryaganj, New Delhi-110002
Visit us at **www.newagepublishers.com**

Preface

"By Education I mean an all-round drawing out of the best in child and man's body, mind and spirit".

M. K. Gandhi

* The book does not claim any originality. **METHODICAL ANALYSIS OF EDUCATION** has been compiled in accordance with the syllabus prescribed by the Department of Education, Rajiv Gandhi University, Dibrugarh University, Gauhati University for the students of B.A., B.Ed., M.A., M.Ed., M.Phil. and Research Courses.
* The highlighting object of the title is to provide a Text cum Refresher for the students dealing with all the relevant topics of Education.
* The language is quite idiomatic, comprehensive, simple, lucid and easy to understand with innovative style. My endeavour has been two fold : a student should be able to grasp the facts and also cultivate in him curiosity to read texts of merit.
* I am very thankful to Mr. Satish Sharma, Branch Manager, Guwahati on behalf of New Age International (P) Ltd. Publishers for undertaking the publication of the book and also to my wife Aditi Deka Pathak and Mr. Piyush Bhengra for their valuable suggestions in writing this title.
* The title is based on almost all the standard works. Though an effort has been made to make the book useful in all respects, yet valuable suggestion to improve the book from all sides will be highly welcomed.

GUPTAJIT PATHAK

Syllabus

GAUHATI UNIVERSITY

B.A. Course, Paper - 1

EDUCATION (General and Major Courses) **Total Marks - 100**

PRINCIPLES AND THEORIES OF EDUCATION

1. Education: Meaning, definition and scope.
2. Aims of Education: Individual, social, liberal and vocational aim of education, Aims of education in democracy.
3. Type of Education: Formal, informal, non-formal, functions and importance of formal and informal agencies, mass-media, distance and continuing education, correspondence course.
4. School - Its functions and responsibilities, school as an agency of social change, Reciprocal relationship between school and community.
5. Home and School - Their relationship ways for better relationship. Co-ordination of activities by school towards total development of the child.
6. Curriculum - Concept, definition, need of curriculum in the school system, defects of curriculum, construction of curriculum in the school system, defects of curriculum, construction of curriculum for primary and secondary school levels, co-relation of studies - its advantages and weakness, types of co-relation, co-curricular activities, needs and importance of such activities in education, types of activities and related advantages.
7. Discipline - Meaning, concept, needs, definitions, principles, role of punishment and reward, freedom and discipline, concept of free discipline, Principles of freedom in modern methods of teaching.
8. Education for aesthetic, moral and spiritual values.
9. Play and play way - Theories, methods and utility - Play way movement in education.
10. Education for leisure - Meaning and needs, importance of leisure.
11. Relation between Philosophy and Education. Major schools of philosophy: Idealism, Naturalism and Existentialism, Pragmatism - their influence on education.
12. Education for the exceptional children, gifted and backward.
13. Education for national integration and international understanding, Education and Globalization.

B.Ed. Course, Paper - 1

PHILOSOPHICAL AND SOCIOLOGICAL FOUNDATIONS OF EDUCATION

Total Marks - 100

1. **Concept of Education:** Meaning and aims of education, factors influencing educational aims : Philosophical, Socio-cultural, Political and Economics. Philosophies of education: General acquittance with Idealism, Realism, including Naturalism, Pragmatism and their influence on education.
2. **Our Educational Heritage:** Our common cultural heritage – its compositeness, unity reachness and continuity.

   Constitution of India: Value of democracy, socialism and secularism, constitutional rights and obligations of citizens. Education in ancient and medieval period.
3. **Education and National Development:** Efforts towards educational reconstruction, Swadeshi Movement and educational contribution of Mahatma Gandhi. Evolution of National System of Education—an overview of the recommendations of the Secondary Education Commission and Kothari Commission; National Education Policy, 1986.
4. **Environmental Education :** State environment, causes of pollution, ecological balance and protection of environment and development. Population and development, population and quality of life, promotion of small family norm, the concept and practise of population education.
5. **Education and Social Change:** Meaning of social change, traditions and modernity, equalizing educational opportunity, education for peace, social cohesion and unity, role of education in promoting desired social change and international understanding.
6. **School Community Relationship:** Interdependence of school and community, understanding and working with community, ways and means of coordinating school community functions.
7. **Teaching as a Profession:** The characteristics and demands of teaching profession, professional development and professional ethics. Value oriented education, moral education, role of the teacher in improving general atmosphere in school.

DIBRUGARH UNIVERSITY

B.A. 1st Year, Paper - 10100

PRINCIPLES OF EDUCATION (CORE) Total Marks - 100

(90 Marks for Written and 10 Marks for Internal Assessment)

OBJECTIVES:

1. To develop an understanding.
   - Meaning, nature and scope and aims of education.
   - Major components of education and their relationships.
   - Role of education as an instrument of social change.
2. To develop an understanding about curriculum and evaluation in education.

Unit-I

Meaning, Concepts, Nature and Scope of Education. 18 (10 hours)

1. Meaning, concepts, nature and scope of education.
2. Types of education: Formal, non-formal and informal.
3. Concepts of continuing, adult, distance and open education.

Unit-II

Aims of Education 18 (12 hours)

1. Determinants of aims (Philosophical, Sociological and Economic).
2. Different aims of education (knowledge, vocational, cultural, moral and spiritual, individual and social aims of education, democratic and totalitarian aims of education) aims of education with reference to the future.

Unit-III

Sociological Foundation of Education 18 (12 hours)

1. Meaning, nature and scope of sociology of education.
2. Difference between sociology and educational sociology.
3. Aims and functions of educational sociology.
4. Socialization: Meaning and concept.
5. Education and socialization processes: Co-operation assimilation competition conflict and discipline.

Unit-IV

Education and Social Change 18 (12 hours)

1. Education and modernization.
2. Education and social change.
3. Education as an instrument of economic growth and human resource development.

4. Education for values.
5. Role of education in the development of a new social order.

Unit-V

Concept of Curriculum and Evaluation in Education 18 (16 hours)

1. Definition and modern concepts and principles of curriculum.
2. Need, significance and types of curriculum.
3. National curriculum.
4. Meaning and need of evaluation.
5. Evaluation and examination.
6. Techniques (written, oral and practical) and tools (test, questionnaire, cumulative records and observation schedule) of evaluation.
7. Continuous and comprehensive evaluation.

B.A. 1st Year, Paper - 10100

PHILOSOPHICAL AND SOCIOLOGICAL FOUNDATIONS OF EDUCATION (MAJOR)

Total Marks - 100

(90 Marks for Written and 10 Marks for Internal Assessment)

OBJECTIVES:

1. To develop undertaking of the meaning, aims, objectives and functions of education.
2. To develop an understanding of the roles of Philosophy and Sociology in education.
3. To develop an understanding of the major components in education and their relationship.
4. To develop knowledge of the structure and functions of the society and the process of social interaction for a change towards better human relationships.
5. To develop an understanding of the role of education as an agent of social change.

COURSE CONTENTS:

Unit-I

Concept and Scope of Education 18 (12 hours)

1. Meaning, Nature and Scope of Education.
   a. Education as a science.
   b. Education as a social process.
   c. Education as human resource development.
2. Functions of Education.
   a. Individual development (Development of skill, basic knowledge, interest and appreciation).

b. Acquaintance with heritage (Preservation and transmission)
c. Development of human values (Social, moral and aesthetic).
d. Acquisition of skills leading to self-actualization and successful living.
e. Social cohesion and social process.

Unit-II

Philosophical Foundations of Education 18 (12 hours)

1. Philosophy of Education: Meaning, nature, scope and function.
2. Science of Education and Philosophy of Education.
3. Relationship between Education and Philosophy.
4. Principles of some major Schools of Philosophy and their contribution to present day education.
   a. Idealism.
   b. Naturalism.
   c. Realism.
   d. Pragmatism.

Unit-III

Aims and Components of Education 18 (12 hours)

1. Determinants of aims:
   a. Philosophical.
   b. Sociological.
   c. Economic.
2. Different aims of education:
   a. Individual.
   b. Social.
   c. Moral.
   d. Cultural.
   e. Vocational.
3. Educational aims with reference to the future.
4. Concepts of freedom and discipline:
   a. Interrelation between discipline, library and democracy.
   b. Importance of discipline in social life.
5. Components of education and their mutual relationship.
   a. Teacher.
   b. Pupil.
   c. Curriculum: Need, significance and types.
   d. Education institution.
   e. Co-curricular activities.

Unit-IV

Social Foundation of Eduction 18 (12 hours)

1. Meaning, nature and scope of educational sociology.
2. Aims and functions of educational sociology.
3. Need for a sociological approach in education.
4. Education as social heritage.
5. Education and culture.
6. Cultural heritage of India.
7. Social groups : Primary and secondary.
8. Social interaction and social stratification.
9. Social mobility and education.
10. Democracy and education.

Unit-V

Socialization, Social Change and Education 18 (12 hours)

1. Meaning of socialization.
2. Education and socialization process:
   a. Co-operation.
   b. Assimilation.
   c. Competition.
   d. Conflict.
   e. Discipline.
3. Education as an instrument, factor and reflection of social change.
4. Agencies of social change.
   a. Home (as the primary unit of a society).
   b. School (as a social sub-system).
   c. Mass media (as a social means).
5. Role of education in the development of a new social order.
6. Role of community in solving social problems in the field of education.

B.Ed. Course, Paper - 1

EDUCATION IN EMERGING INDIAN SOCIETY

Total Marks - 100

Objectives : To enable the student-teachers understand :

1. About the relationship between philosophy and education and implications of philosophy on education.

2. About the importance and role of education in the progress of Indian society.
3. The need to study education in a sociological perspective and for creation of a new social order as per constitutional directives.
4. About the cultural heritage of India.
5. About the emerging concerns in the field of education.

Syllabus:

Unit-I

Education and Our Heritage: 20

- Our Common Cultural Heritage - Its compositeness, unity, riches and continuity.
- Our Philosophical Traditions - Central teachings of Indian Philosophies viz: Samkhya, Yoga and Vedanta.
- Impact of Idealism, Naturalism and Pragmatism on Indian system of education with reference to Gandhiji, Tagore, Rousseau and Dewey.

Unit-II

Education : Aims and Function 15

- Education: Nature, meaning and scope.
- Functions of education for Indian society.
- The Indian constitution and its directive principles, various articles related to education.
- Modernization - Its operational aspects and education.
- Education in India : National and emotional integration.
- Secularism, democracy and socialistic patterns of society.
- Education as an agency of Human Resource Development.

Unit-III

Education and Indian Society 10

- Indian social system: Structures, class, caste, stratification mobility.
- Role of education in promoting equality of educational opportunity.
- Educational needs of special groups (SC, ST, women, mentally and physically challenged groups).
- Education as a tool of economic development.

Unit-IV

Educational Heritage of India 15

- Development of education in India in historical perspective with regard to aim, Organization, curriculum and method of teaching within the Vedic, Brahmanic, Buddhist and Islamic systems of education.
- Education under colonial rule with reference to Macaulay's Minute, Wood's Despatch, Curzon's Policy and Nationalist movement.

Unit-V

Education and National Development 15

- Educational development during 1947 to 1966.
- Educational development during 1966–1986.
- Educational development since 1986.

Unit-VI

Emerging Concerns for Indian Education 15

- Population education with special emphasis on adolescence education.
- Environmental education.
- Privatization of education.
- Sarva Shiksha Abhiyan.
- Value education in Indian context.

RAJIV GANDHI UNIVERSITY

B.A. 1st Year, Paper - 1
(Pass & Honours)
ELEMENTS OF EDUCATION

OBJECTIVES:

1. To acquaint the students with the basis of education.
2. To familiarize the students with the aims and objectives of education.
3. To develop the awareness among the students about the structure, agencies and other aspects of education.
4. To familiarize the students with the basis of educational technology.

COURSE CONTENTS:

Unit-I

* Concept of Education
* Meaning, Nature and Scope of Education
* Types of Education : Formal and Non-formal

Unit-II

* Aims of Education
* Individual and Social Aims
* Democratic Aims
* Vocational Aims
* Moral and Cultural Aims

Unit-III

* Education Structure
* Educational Ladder
* Secondary Education Commission, Kothari Commission and New Education Policy on the Structure of Education.
* New Pattern of Education (10+2+3)

Unit-IV

* Educational Psychology
* Meaning, Nature and Scope of Educational Psychology
* Methods of Educational Psychology
* Concept of Learning
* Laws of Learning

Unit-V

* Human Growth and Development
* Meaning of Growth and Development
* Heredity and Environment
* Stages of Development
  1. Infancy
  2. Childhood
  3. Adolescence

Unit-VI

* Instincts and Emotion
* Meaning and Definition of Instinct
* Instinct according to McDougal
* Meaning and Definition of Emotion
* Classification of Emotion
* Theories of Emotion
  1. Central Theory of Emotion
  2. The James Langue Theory of Emotion
  3. Educational Utility of Instincts and Emotion

Unit-VII

* Educational Technology
* Meaning, Nature and Scope of Educational Technology
* Types of Educational Technology – Hardware and Software
* Utility of Educational Technology in Formal and Non-formal Education
* Limitations of Educational Technology with reference to India

Unit-VIII

* Educational Sociology
* Meaning, Nature and Scope of Educational Sociology
* Socialization

Unit-IX

* Education and Modernization
* Concept of Modernization
* Constituents and Indicators of Modernization
* Impact of Education on Modernization
* National Integration

B.Ed. Course

Paper - 1 : EDUCATIONAL PSYCHOLOGY Total Marks - 100

OBJECTIVES:

1. To develop in students an understanding of the rich philosophical, social, cultural and educational heritage of India.
2. To acquaint the students with the traditional and contemporary values of the Indian society.
3. To make the students familiar with the significant educational thoughts of some of the leading thinkers – Western and Indian.
4. To help students realize the professional role of teachers towards national development and social transformation.

COURSE OUTLINE

Unit-1

Indian Traditions and Values

- Philosophical Tradition.
- Purusartha - Dharma, Artha, Kama, Moksha
- Doctrine of "Nishkama Karma"
- Idealism with reference to Plato.
- Naturalism with reference to Rabindranath Tagore, Dewey Instrumentation and Experimentation.
- Humanism—Historical, Scientific and Buddhist.
- Philosophy and Education.
- Significance of Philosophy for Educational Practice.
- Meaning, Nature and Scope of Education.

Unit-2

Thoughts in Education

- India – M. K. Gandhi and Basic Education.
- Rabindranath Tagore and Viswa Bharati.
- Swami Vivekananda and Man Making Education.
- Western – Rousseau, John Dewey, J.F. Harbert.

Unit-3

Constitutional Provisions of Education

- Principles of Equality, Justice, Socialism, Democracy, Freedom, Secularism and their implications for Education.
- Human Rights Education - Education for all, Concept of Human Rights. Human Rights and Indian Values, Education for Human Rights, Education as Fundamental Rights.

Unit-4

Education and Social Change

- Social change – Meaning and factors, Education as an instrument of social change, Modernization.
- National and emotional integration and International understanding.

Unit-5

Teaching as a Profession

- Status of teaching as a profession.
- Professional ethics of a teacher.
- Professional hazards in teaching, recruitment and career promotion.
- Profile of a good teacher.
- Teacher as a leader in the class and in the community.
- Emergence of NCTE and its role for Quality Teacher Education.

Practicum

Any one out of the following:

1. Critical analysis of any significant thought (thinker) in Education and preparing a report thereof.
2. Survey of an educational institution/programme and preparing a report.
3. Designing a curriculum for any particular level or class with an analysis of the present one and preparing a report.
4. Survey of the social attitude towards teachers and preparing a report.
5. Preparation of a self-appraisal/peer group appraisal format and report.
6. Preparation of report on any innovative idea on Education/Teaching/Teacher/Student etc.
7. Preparation of a report on ways and means of infusing work experience into the training programme.
8. Preparation of a report on problems and prospects of Teacher Education in Arunachal Pradesh/North East.

EVALUATION SCHEME

1. Session work : 20 marks
2. Written examination : 80 marks
3. Duration : 3 hours

The examination paper will have 5 questions with internal choice. Each question carries equal marks.

Assignment for BHARATIYA SHIKSHA PARISHAD

MASTER OF EDUCATION PROGRAMME (M.Ed.)

Philosophical & Sociological Foundations of Education

Paper - 1

Note : Attempt any five questions from each part.

PART - A

1. Discuss the importance of education in human life.
2. Discuss the need and origin of formal agencies of education.
3. Discuss the broad and narrow meaning of education.
4. How can you say that "State" is an informal agency of education? Give reasons.
5. Should the state control education? Give arguments for your answer.
6. Why is it necessary for a teacher to consider the aims of education?
7. What do you understand by education for intellectual development? Explain.
8. How can education help in promoting inter-cultural feeling in India?
9. What should be the aims of education in a democratic society?
10. Point out the dangers of narrow. What type of nationalism was present in ancient India.

PART - B

1. What is meant by Naturalism? How has it influenced the theory of education?
2. Explain the nature of discipline and the image of teacher from the idealistic stand point in education.
3. What are the fundamental principles of pragmatism?
4. What are the aims of education according to Rabindranath Tagore?
5. Give a critical estimate of educational thought of Rabindranath Tagore.
6. What are the aims of education according to Mahatma Gandhi?
7. Describe the salient features of Gandhiji's method of teaching.
8. Discuss the relationship between discipline and freedom in education.
9. What are the modern trends in education?
10. What is meant by social change? What is the role of education in the process?

Contents

1

Education with Its Pivotal Scenario

"Education means bringing out of the ideas of universal validity which are latent in the mind of every man".

Socrates

In every civilized society men and women believe that education is comprehensive, compulsory and necessary for every individual. Education is an important human activity. The every concept of education is like a diamond which appears to be of a different colour when seen from different angles.

ETHNOLOGICAL DEFINITION

The word 'Education' had its origin in the Latin word 'Educatum', which itself is composed of two words, 'E' and 'Duco'. It means developing and progressing. Hence, in its literal scenario, education means becoming develop or progressing from inside to outside. In other words, education implies some of the changes for the better and greater in a person.

DIFFERENT EDUCATIONAL THEORISTS HAVE GIVEN DIFFERENT DERIVATIONS OF THE CONCEPT '*EDUCATION*'

1. According to **Froebel,** *"Education is a process through which child makes its internal and external".*
2. According to **Eddison,** *"When education works on noble mind it draws out to view every latent virtue and perfection".*
3. According to **Pestalozzi,** *"Education is defined as natural, harmonious and progressive development of men's innate powers".*
4. According to **M. K. Gandhi,** *"I mean all-round drawing out of the best in child and man's body, mind and spirit".*

Education is aggregate of all the processes by which a person develops ability, attitudes and behaviour of practical values in the society in which he lives.

NARROW SENSE OF EDUCATION

In large majority of people use the concept of education is to mean the training undertaken for some years in some educational institutions. This is the narrow meaning of the concept of education. In other words, it implies education provided according to a fixed curriculum by a particular set of people in a specific place.

WIDER SENSE OF EDUCATION

The very betterment of an adjusted pattern of life is the product of that educational system. The very educative system is going on every moment in the life of a person. Here, each day's activities have an effect upon him. The educant may perceive or not perceive that effect.

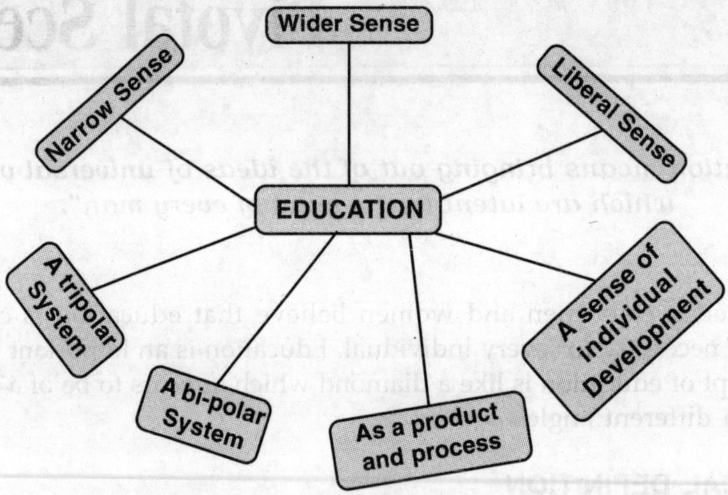

Fig. 1. Basic Areas of Education

LIBERAL SENSE OF EDUCATION

When the word 'Education' is accepted in its more literal meaning it is granted that all the times and places the individual is imbibing some of its areas. Here, it is not limited merely to the classroom. It can be obtained in all kinds of social organizations, associations, individuals, nature, etc. Its mention may be made that a child gets his education not only from his teacher, but also from the entire environment of his life.

A SENSE OF INDIVIDUAL DEVELOPMENT

Education is the complete development of the individuality of the child. According to some thinkers and philosophers, education is nothing but a process which a child can have free, spontaneous and individual betterment. Basically, the main achievement of 'education' lies in ability to arouse interest towards the subject of inspiring him.

AS A PRODUCT AND PROCESS

Education is the product of learning process. It implies growth and development. Education is a process or system through which date, experience and information are achieved. Of course, it is a continuous and comprehensive process of training and guidance.

A BI-POLAR SYSTEM

Education, of course, is a bi-polar system. Here, it involves the interplay of the educator and the educant. In this process of education the teacher and the taught are the active participants. So, education is nothing but a bi-polar process by which the natural, spontaneous and progressive betterment of the child is justified.

A TRI-POLAR SYSTEM

Education is also a tri-polar system. It involves the interaction of the personality of the educator and the educant in a social setting. In other words, it affects the modification of the behaviour of the educant.

EDUCATION IN THE WEST

Educational training like every other branch of knowledge started in the philosophical deliberation of the ancient Greek philosophers. Here, mention may be made of Plato's name. He termed education as a "Life long process starting from the first years of childhood and lasting to the very end of the life".

EDUCATION IN INDIA

In Indian approach, it becomes necessary to cover the spiritual area. Here, it is accepted as a part of betterment by education. In other words, Indian philosophers have placed special importance upon this. According to Shankaracharya, "Education is that which leads salvation". Yajnavalkya said that, only that is education which gives a sterling character to an individual and renders him useful for the world.

A modern developed society cannot survive without education. It is as old as humanity. It helps people adjust to change. Succinctly, it is only education which can help a person understanding to all the social changes and providing the skills and technology for adjusting to them.

The concept of education is like a diamond which appears to be of different colours (natures) when seen from different angles. Education being an important social activity, its meanings have been changing through the ages, due to changes in social and physical conditions.

The general idea about what education actually means is called the concept of education.

Education has been explained as the sum total of experiences of life. Since life is changing under an evolutionary process along with the environment and social structure, the concept of education also changes with the changes of area. As such, we find different terms of education.

In the primitive age, informal education was given. Hence, it was very simple. The fundamental feature was the actual participation in social, cultural and economic activities and the following of the directions of the senior members of the family. In that particular period education meant aptitude and skill in procuring food, clothes and self protection.

In ancient India, the main concept of education was self-realization which was to be attained through self-denial and formation of character.

2

Concept of Education

The vital concept of education is like a diamond which appears to be of a different colour (nature) when seen from different angles or point of view or philosophy of life.

Philosophy in Sanskrit or Hindi is known as ***'Darshan'*** which means knowledge of the truth. ***'Darshan'*** has been derived from the Sanskrit root **'Chris'** which means **'to see'**. It has also been called metaphysics (Tatuajyan) meaning, the knowledge of the real of truth. So, both the combined will mean **"truth knowledge"** or **"reliable knowledge"** which is generally gained by seeing.

BROAD MEANING OF EDUCATION

The word **'Education'** makes it clear that this method is broad-based. From birth up to death we come in contact with many things, persons, institutions and ideas.

In this broad sense, experiences gained from excursions, marriage ceremonies, social organizations and fairs come under the term **'Education'.**

In this broad sense, every individuals is both a teacher and a taught. The state teaches us through its propaganda and institutions. We learn something by participating in religious programmes. Our education goes on during our travels also.

The idea of lifelong education has challenged the traditional concept of terminal education. Education now lasts throughout life from cradle to the grow so that it could meet the needs of individuals and of society as a whale.

The important concept of lifelong education was given by UNESCO in its meeting in 1965. The basic principle was defined as continuing throughout an individual's life from his earliest childhood to the end of his days.

NARROW MEANING OF EDUCATION

a. In the narrower sense, education is confined to a few specific influence which have a bearing on the development of the child. These influences have been deliberately planned, chosen and employed by the community for the welfare of the younger generation. These influences aim at modifying the behaviour of the child, making him different from what he would have been without education.

b. To quote T. Raymont, in legal enactments, education does not include self-culture and the general influences of one's surroundings, but only these special influences which are consciously and designedly brought to bear upon the younger by the adult portion of the community, whether through the family, the church or the state.

EDUCATION AS A CONTINUOUS AND COMPREHENSIVE PROCESS

a. Education is a process through which human personality develops. It is not a temporary process which begins at a definite time and comes to an end at particular point in the life of man.

b. Education begins at the time of birth; not only has this, according to some psychologists it begins even before birth.

c. Education is a process that goes a throughout life, and is promoted by almost every experience in life.

IS EDUCATION A SCIENCE OR AN ART?

a. When we take the narrow meaning of education, we naturally think whether it is a science or an art. Arts are after inborn, such as the art of poetry.

b. Art is also a source of pleasure to man. Man by nature is interested in arts.

c. Education is undoubtedly an art but, it also a science. Education has its own science. It has its own principles.

d. It helps develop child's interests and abilities in education. We come to know the theory of teaching a particular subject through the science of education.

DEFINITIONS OF EDUCATION

a. *Education is something which makes man self-relevant and self-less.* **Rig-Veda**

b. *Education is for liberalization.* **Upanishad**

c. *Human education means the training which one gets from nature.* **Panini**

d. *By education I mean all around drawing out the best in the child and man's body mind and spirit.*
M.K. Gandhi

e. *Creation of sound mind in a sound body.* **Aristotle**

f. *I mean by education that training which is given by suitable habits to the first instincts if virtue in children.* **Plato**

g. *Education is the creation of a sound mind in sound body.* **Aristotle**

h. *Education is a natural, harmonious and progressive development of man's innate powers.*
Pestalozzi

i. *Education is a conscious and deliberate process in which are personality acts upon another in under of modify the developments of the other by the communication and manipulation and knowledge.* **Adams**

j. *Education is the development of good moral character.* **Herbart**

k. *Education is the development of all those capacities in the individual which enable him to control his environments and fulfil his possibilities.* **John Dewey**

l. *Education should be thought of as the process of man's reciprocal adjustment to nature, to his fellows, and to the ultimate nature of the cosmos.* **H Horne**

m. *Education means the universal distribution of accent knowledge.* **Leste F. Ward**

SCOPE

Education is a supplementary process of life. Entire life of man is the scope of education. The scope of education will be the entire field of life of man and the problems of education will be the problems of life.

Education now treated as a separate discipline, still in developing stage. Following are the main division of education :

EDUCATIONAL PHILOSOPHY

Philosophic ideologies have been found particularly significant in the aims of education and their evaluation.

EDUCATIONAL SOCIOLOGY

Besides, relationship between culture and education, society and education, and main elements and process of socialization are also studied.

HISTORY OF EDUCATION

Education is a lifelong process. The history of education helps in knowing the early educational thoughts and in scheming different educational problems.

TEACHING METHODS

For different subjects, different teaching methods are required though there may be some common thing in then. It mainly discusses the nature of teaching of different subjects, need and aims of teaching etc.

EDUCATIONAL ADMINISTRATION

The educational system of a nation depends very much on the administration of education. In this branch establishment of schools, their management, supervision and control, their inspection system, appointment of managers, teachers, principals and their employees, their salary and allowances, their working condition etc. are studied.

EDUCATIONAL PROBLEMS

This branch studies the different problems for finding their solution.

It occurred main problems at different levels of education and their remedies, their basic courses and means of remaining them, administration and control by the government, its relative merits and demerits etc.

COMPARATIVE EDUCATION

This branch makes a comparative study of the educational systems of other countries. In the study of comparative education, steps are also made to know the influence of cultural, social, political and economic conditions on the educational trait of a country.

FUNCTIONS

Education is defined and claimed as natural, harmonious and progressive development of man's innate powers. It is an important agent to bring about progressive ideas. It may be said that education is as old as the history of human civilization.

INDIVIDUAL FUNCTION

a. The main function of education is to reform the body and mind of a child to adopt himself to the environmental forces. The child should take the opportunity of making this individual adjustment.

b. Every child is immature at birth. He is to be deliberately trained for affective growth of life and social intercourse by a mature person.

c. Every child tries to adjust himself to his environments. He learns a lot in his family and also from his own experience in the family and in the neighbourhood.

d. The individual adjustment of a number of a people can also bring about certain changes in environment may be it social or political.

SOCIAL FUNCTION

a. The primary function of education relates to social development. Life is an Inseparable unit of society. As such, all individual development must have a bearing in the society.

b. The function of education may be conservative and relative.

c. At the same time, education brings about social progress by creation of progressive ideas.

d. Education has a creative function too.

e. According to John Dewey, "Education is primarily related to the reorganization of human experience."

f. Changes of far reaching national and international importance are taking place and new problems are facing the citizen every day.

g. Child is active by nature. He must be busy in one activity or the other and this activity learns to his growth.

FUNCTION OF EDUCATION IN NATIONAL LIFE

National progress depends upon the hard work energy, selflessness and devotion of the individual. Hence, an individual cannot be separated from his nation.

a. The vital function of education in national life is to make the rising generation understand its rights and duties as individual citizens of democratic set up.

b. **Secondly,** a successful functioning of democracy needs efficient leadership in all spheres of social, political, religious and educational activities.

c. **Thirdly**, India is basically a land of diversities. Hence, it is the function of education to bring unity in this vast diversity. Then only the best and importance of the nation can be served and protected.

d. **Fourthly,** educational integration leads to national integration. We have to raise our people from local narrow prejudices of caste, community, religion and provincialism to a broad national outlook. Really speaking, it is the domain of education.

THREE PROMINENT FUNCTION OF EDUCATION

Modern thinkers have spelt out three prominent functions of education. They are

a. **Conservative,** i.e. preserving all the old traditions, values, ideals, worthwhile customs and way of living.

b. **Transmitive,** i.e. transmitting the cultural heritage to the younger generation, and Progressive, i.e. reconstructing new experiences transmitted, should be simplified, purified, and balanced. In the present scenario, a complex social order, the experiences given, must be reached and balanced.

CONCEPT OF NON-FORMAL EDUCATION

The non-formal education programme is a massive programme expected to cover 70 percent of the population of children of the age group 6-14. Hence, the cost factor is a very important point to keep in mind in developing the NEP programme.

Non-formal education is an arrangement wherein flexibility is the key word. The system is an open one with regard to various aspects of education, i.e. admissions, curriculum place of instructions and the time and duration of instruction. Open University, open learning and the correspondence or distance learning courses are the various examples of such a system.

IMPORTANT FEATURES OF NON-FORMAL EDUCATION

Although non-formal education has emerged as the only alternative strategy in our case to supplement the formal education, this is the only alternative in the rich countries also to compliment the formal system with the view to continually equip the workers with the latest knowledge and technology in the trades they are engaged in according to Professor Malcolm's Adiseshiah, "the non-formal education is wide-ranging because it comprehends all learning outside."

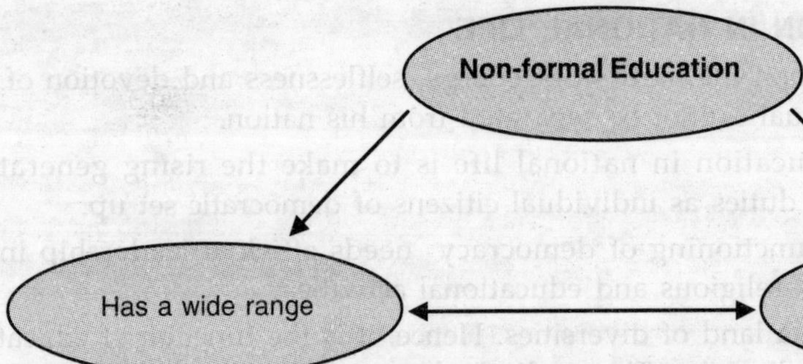

Fig. 2. Non-formal Education

All learning outside of the formal system and has no parameters of time and space. Non-formal education has not developed or evolved in its own philosophical understandings. It merely furnishes condition under which an individual puts challenge to societal fate as it were.

The very concept of non-formal education can be designed as the following ways :

a. Non-formal education is a multifaceted process.
b. It is designed not only for the children and youth and also for the adults who at any age may have a desire to learn.
c. It is an open system of education without rigid rules and regulations and fixed stages of time schedules.
d. It prepares the learners for active life and objective work.
e. It educates the learners to adopt.

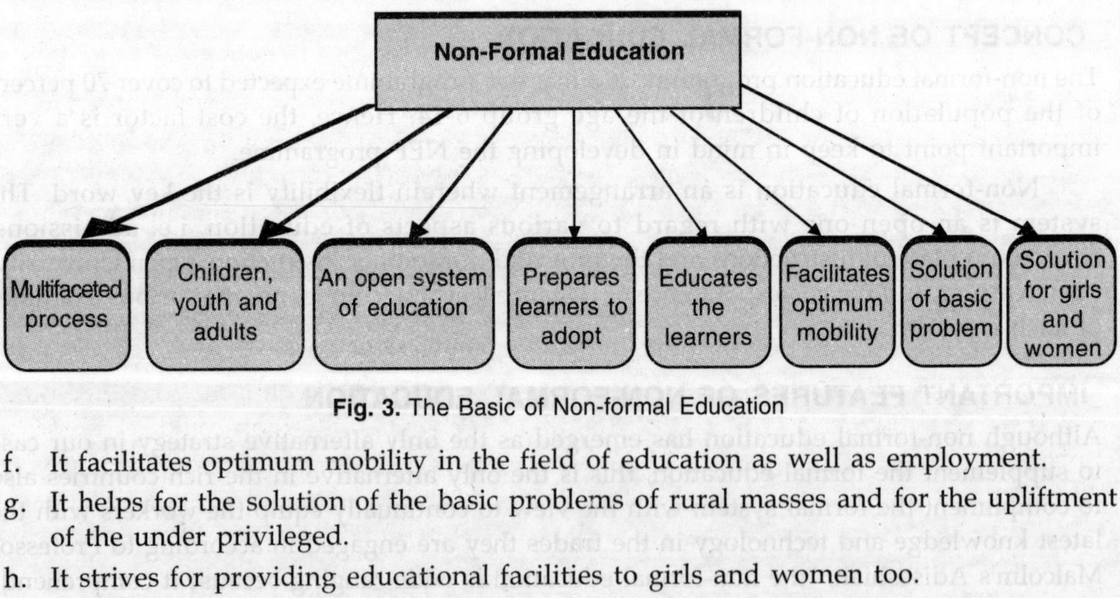

Fig. 3. The Basic of Non-formal Education

f. It facilitates optimum mobility in the field of education as well as employment.
g. It helps for the solution of the basic problems of rural masses and for the upliftment of the under privileged.
h. It strives for providing educational facilities to girls and women too.

NON-FORMAL EDUCATION IN INDIAN SCENARIO

THE NEED AND SIGNIFICANCE OF NON-FORMAL EDUCATION IN NATIONAL DEVELOPMENT

Over the last few years, the term non-formal education has gained currency in India in view of its importance in developing necessary knowledge, attitudes and skill in the vast section of the population which could not make use of the formal system of education.

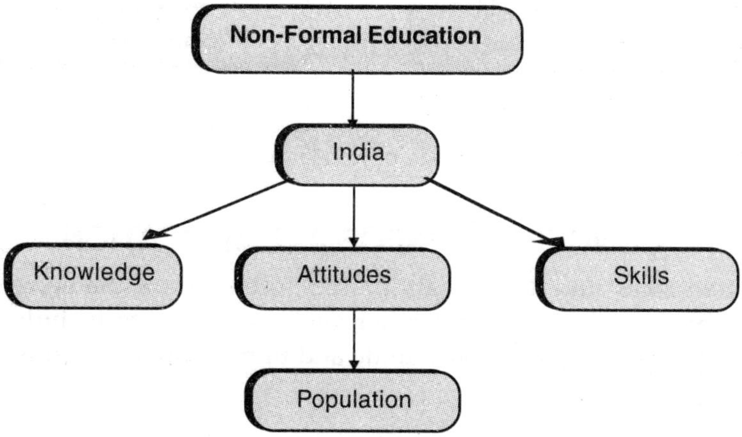

Fig. 4. Non-formal Education

It cannot departure from the existing pattern of full time schooling in order to meet the needs of that section of the population which finds it difficult to take advantages of the existing facilities of education.

Non-formal education as an alternative pattern of education caters to the need of both adults and children. The programme for the adults needs a re-orientation to reflect the emerging needs. Promotions of such programmes which have a quick pay-self have to receive precedence over literacy.

Equal importance has also to be giving to non-formal education for children. Unlike the adults, the needs here are two fold; the first is to help those children who desire to join the formal set up education for certificate-oriented courses or higher studies to cover, within the shortest possible time, the courses that their counterparts have covered in the formal education.

It is observed that the needs of the different groups even within the some age range would vary from place to place. Programmes of functional education could of course, be common to a great extent for almost all the groups.

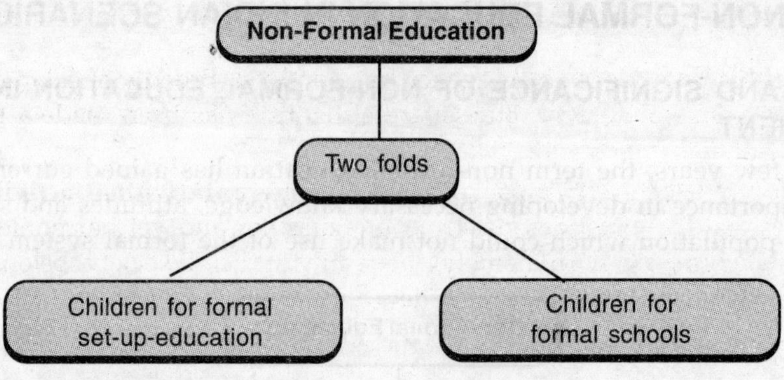

Fig. 5. The Folds of Non-formal Education

CONCEPT OF INFORMAL EDUCATION

Informal education takes into its orbit all indirect influences of the home and the society. The press, the libraries, the films and other such agencies are included as agencies of informal education. Their influences are subtle and imperceptible but at the same time very important and significant.

HIGHLIGHTING OBJECTIVES OF INFORMAL EDUCATION

a. It has no definite aim.
b. It is not imported through any formal lesson or well planned means.
c. There is no such definite course and period.
d. They are not conscious of the process.
e. No organized agency is behind this process.
f. It is a life-long process. It has no start and no end.
g. It is natural and therefore it does not strain anybody.

DIFFERENT AGENCIES OF INFORMAL EDUCATION FAMILY

FAMILY IS THE FUNDAMENTAL UNIT OF SOCIETY

It generally consists of husband, wife and their children. In ancient society, servants were also regarded as members of family. These servants were rather very important members.

Etymologically, the word **'family'** is derived from the word **'famulus'** which means servants. Apart from these, a join family in India comprises other members like uncles, aunts, the in-laws.

To quote T. Raymont, " *During the earliest and moist impressionable years, the family is the child, entire social environment; and though the social circle widens when he goes to school and begins to form outside friendships, yet the family remains for some years the largest and most central portion of the circle."*

SOCIETY

Society has get his own place as an agency of education. Broadly speaking, family should be regarded as a unit of society. But separate mention has been made a family as it has got great educational importance.

"Education is essentially a social and not a mere individual activity". Now there are three necessary societies, distinct from one another and yet harmoniously combined by God, into which man is born: namely, the family and civil society, belong to the natural order, the church to the supernatural order.

THE SPECIFIC DUTIES

The following are the main duties of the society as an educational institution:

a. To establish schools for securing its culture and passing it on to the next generation.

b. To give the knowledge relationship between the individual and society.

c. To get him to familiarizes himself with various units of society like family, association, and nation and to provide knowledge of their mutual relationship.

d. To provide knowledge of social traditions, values, ideas and belief to the members of society.

e. To help acquaint children with various social activities like the organization of fairs, participation in celebrations and ceremonies, holding conferences, meeting people in fairs and so on.

f. To provide a knowledge of political, economic and religious factors of society.

STATE

State is also an informal agency of education. The relationship between the state and education in a separate chapter, the proper management of education is an important task of the state.

Apart from school, family and society state also educates us as an informal agency of education. People always learn something all the other from the state without any definite rule, place or time.

Briefly the main duties of the state as an educational agency are given as under:

a. Instead of taking the place of the individual and the family, the state should help in the development of both.

b. It is the duty of the state to establish its own schools and provide assistance to private schools.

c. State is responsible for the change in the form of schools according to needs.

d. State is to establish inter-relationship among various agencies of education.

e. State should keep education free form local crises by allowing some local elements of participate in the process of education, but subordinating them to the national system of education.

f. It should provide sound attitude to parents towards education.

g. Proper arrangement of training for teachers is to be made by the state so that the standard of education may not fall.

h. State is expected to help inculcate feeling of duty to the nation in the minds of its citizens and it should contribute in the development of moral ideas for social efficiency.

According to M. K. Gandhi, *"The state should perform its functions with the minimum use of coercion"*. It was to rule **"through its moral authority based upon the greatest goodwill of the people"**. Hence, state can function effectively as an agency of education when it performs its functions with the use of violence only if it is inevitable.

RELIGION

E.D. Burton defined, *"Religion and education are natural allies. Both recognize and have to do with spiritual as our against exclusive attention to the physical and material. Both seek to emancipate man, not from contact with his environment, but form slowing to is, to enlarge his horizon and quicken his aspirations"*.

Religion may be defined as the belief in a supernatural reality which affects the believer emotionally in such a way as to impel him to perform certain acts directed towards the supernatural reality.

The word **'religion'** has its origin in two Latin words -**'re'** and **'legew'**, meaning to **'bind back'**. Explaining this thing, Gisbert writes, **"Religion establishes a double bond, one between man and good and the other between man and men children of god."**

OTHER IMPORTANT AGENCIES

Sports : Children are naturally interested in games. Adults are also interested in play. By means of games and sports feelings of cooperation honesty and love are developed in children. This is also an important informal agency of education. Sports, games and athletics play an pivotal part in the educational life of the school. Besides, the academic progress of the students the school must pay attention towards the physical well-being of students. A sound mind can only flourish in a sound body.

Field Trips and Excursion: Provisions should be made for field trips and excursion. It is said that best way of knowing a thing intimately is to observe and to see it. Field trips provide this opportunity.

Educational trips can be of varied interest of field trips and excursions are properly planned and organized. There should also be needed follow-up of these field trips and excursions to secure their curriculum advantage. They should not degenerate into divisions.

School Magazines and Publications: School magazines and publications are also important part of the academic life of the school. It is also an informal agency of education. These publications may be the farm of news bulletins, wall-magazines, school magazines or an annual report.

The educational value of these school magazines and publication is really great. They provide channel of expressions among them. It should be enthused to improve the tone of the school and the quality of its various curricular and co-curricular activities.

Films: Children learn many things from the films. Adolescent boys and girls learn about modes of fashion from films. It is said that even the people of non-Hindi speaking states has learn among Hindi film songs.

Adolescents learn very soon the dialogues spoken by the heroes and heroines in the films, people also listen to the message of the actors. Films can promote social welfare if they screen good stories and adopt techniques suiting the needs of society.

Radio: In our daily life we learn some things from radio programmes. We receive sufficient education from the speeches on different subjects delivered by great scholars. Now the radio programme organizers sometime arrange for well planned education to be imparted to different age groups of people.

Television: Television and films are mass media which are both visual and auditory in nature about which we will discuss now. Radio and television although relatively new media, these sources have already made their impression on world civilization very strikingly.

The role of television in the education has been well established. Our experience of SITE (Satellite Instructional Television Experiments) in 1975-76 has indicated that acceptance of community television was found to be quite high in rural area.

Press: The modern society has been too complex to function only through direct communication between one individual and another. Most of our important messages must reach many people at a time in order to be effective and meaningful.

We get some new experience by reading daily newspaper, weekly papers, fortnightly and monthly magazines, annual or half yearly journals and various bulletins.

Library and Reading Room: Libraries and reading rooms provide education by making available various papers, journals, magazines, great reference books and books on many subjects for reference and study.

Social Education Centre: Under community development project social education centre have been established at villages and mahals of cities. We informally receive education from these centres.

Youth Programme: We also get education from the programmes of youth organization which organize different types of education activities.

Scouting and Girl-Guiding: Scouting and girl guiding programmes provide education to boys and girls respectively both are informal agencies of education. All schools must encourage boy scouting and girls guiding the advantages of scouting and girl guiding are many.

National Service Scheme: To involve student youths during their vacations in constructive work, certain large scale campaign programmes have been organized, as part of N.S.S. in the course of which certain aspects of rural needs are covered.

National Cadet Camp: Learning the last few years the Government of India has instituted the junior division of the National Cadet Corps which is open to pupils of all schools. The officers are drawn largely from the teaching profession. This has the advantage of bringing teachers and pupils into closure and contact in the training camps.

Museum: Only a brief reference needs to be made to museums as an informal agency of education in India, until well affair in dependence museum played an insignificant role in disseminating information's and as centres of education.

3

Aims of Education

INDIVIDUAL AIM OF EDUCATION

The importance of aims in education has been emphasized by scholar, philosophers and educators through all ages. Education must have aims as **"activity with on aims in all one with acting intelligently"**. In a simple sentence, **"Individuality is the ideal of life"**.

a. The aim of education is self-realization by the individual. Self realization implies the harmonious development of the faculties of the individual.

b. When one has achieved self realization, he has an inquiring mind, knowledge of health, habits, intellectual and aesthetic interests, character and ability to read efficiently, write effectively and speak his language fluently.

c. The individual aim in education therefore recognizes the claims of the person to develop his potential powers.

d. Education is essentially a process of adjustment. In this process, sometimes the activity of the individual dominates and sometimes the social forces prevail. It has been observed that each factor tends to subordinate the other at all times. This has led to the conflicting views of the individuals and social aims of education.

e. The supporters of the individual aim look upon the individual as an independent unit which forms the society or state. Individual, not the society, should be given priority.

f. **According to Nunn,** *"Nothing good can enter the human would accept through the few activities of men and women. Every individual has the right to acquire development freely and to realize the highest potentialities of the self"*.

g. Environment and atmosphere influence the individual and affect the traits necessary for the development of personality.

h. In ancient Greece emphasis was given on the all round development of the individual. This is the reason why he attained a radical development in all spheres of civilization — art, literature, science and philosophy, unlike Sparta which only developed proficiency in physical culture and war.

i. School of every type fulfil their purpose so far as they foster the few growth of individuality.

j. The good of society lies in training the individual to the octant of bringing out all that is best in his being.

HIGHLIGHTING STANDPOINTS

The development of individuality has been emphasized by all the type of thinkers-Naturalists, Biologists, psychologists, Moralists and all Progressive thinkers.

THE NATURALISTS STANDPOINT

Research, the naturalist sow the early seeds of individual aim in his writings. According to him man and citizen can be trained simultaneously.

THE BIOLOGICAL STANDPOINT

The Biologists say every creature is a unique product and making a continuous effort to reach perfection. Education must give strength to this effort, by fully developing the individual self of aim.

THE PSYCHOLOGICAL STANDPOINT

When Pestalozzi declared that education should be psychologies means that education must be individualized as no two children are alike in their inborn capabilities psychologists and biological findings view that the ultimate good of society like in discovering the hidden value of the individual.

THE MORAL STANDPOINT

The Moralists also believe that every individual is capable of doing good or evil, according to I as he has been trained, education should lead the individual to the good of perfection.

INDIVIDUAL AS THE SOCIAL PROGRESS

Education is meant to push the wheel of social progress forward it must allow the free development of individual man and women. It should create conditions "Under which individuality is completely developed.

CRITICISM

a. The exaggerated claim of the individual may have an adverse effect on the collective welfare of the society. As Raymont has observed, "*an individual is only a figment of imagination. An individual cannot be conceived in isolation from society*".

b. The exponents of the individual aim hold that a good society or a good state can be formed only when its individuals attain the fullest development of their individuality.

c. Every individual have a separate entity of his own. As such, it should be duty of the society to offer for individual perfection.

d. Individual cannot be regarded as an instrument to reach a goal. Instead of individual, society should be an instrument to attain individual's personality.
e. It is also observed that an individual has an infinite value and this value ultimately become the value of the society itself.
f. Education helps the individual to frame his original contribution to the variegated whole of human life as his nature permits.
g. To some extent, the individual aim, in its extreme form is undesirable. Because, it makes a person selfish and self centered.
h. To some extent it ignores Socio-cultural influence.
i. It ignores rich heritage.
j. Each one of us has individuality as a self sufficient unit. But, this individuality is to be transformed into personality to make it fit for living in society.

CONCEPT OF VOCATIONAL AIM IN EDUCATION

Vocational aim in education implies preparing an individual for earning this livelihood. It is basically concerned with enabling an individual to prepare for a productive work rather than for a clerical work. Technical aspects rather than academic and intellectual objects are given more importance in such a type of vocational education.

DEMOCRACY AND EMPHASIS TO VOCATIONAL AIM

One of the most important objectives of education in a democracy is to prepare socially efficient individuals and without vocational education, an individual cannot be socially efficient. In the words of M.K. Gandhiji, "True Education ought to be for them (boys and girls) a kind of insurance against unemployment."

The vocational aim trains an individual to be self-sufficient and not a drag or a parasite on society.

Democracy indicates that education should be useful rather than ornamental. It would be wrong to call the vocational aim as purely a **'Bread and Butter Aim.'** A vocational trained individual is not devoid of human feelings.

Indian education system has been often criticized that the vocational aim of education remained neglected during the British period. Lack of vocational element led to the backwardness of Indian economy and reduced opportunities for employment. Purely bookish knowledge deprived us of the fruit of industrial development.

VOCATIONAL AIM IN EDUCATION HAS THE FOLLOWING STANDPOINTS :

a. It relates education to productivity.
b. It makes an individual for a better job.
c. It broadens one's horizon.
d. It inculcates dignity of labour.
e. It gives opportunities to the maximum utilization of the material resources of the country.

HIGHLIGHTING CRITICISM OF THE VOCATIONAL AIM IN EDUCATION

a. It is argued that life is more that bread and butter, man is not merely to earn his livelihood in this world. Earning a living is too important a part of an individual's life to be neglected but it is only a part.

b. An individual has to develop himself intellectually, morally and socially. He has social obligations to discharge.

c. He has leisure time to be utilized profitably. A purely vocational aim narrows down one's outlook on life. He enables an individual to be a good mechanic, a good doctor, a good lawyer, a good electrician, but necessarily not a good man.

BALANCED VIEW

a. General or Liberal education is one and the same thing: Vocational or Technical education also means nearly the same. A distinction between Liberal and Vocational education is made on the following grounds

b. Liberal education is supposed to be connected with cultural and academic aspects of education while vocational education means specific training for a particular vocation.

INDIVIDUALITY

a. Nunn makes clear his point by saying that individuality is not the state of being individual or having separate existence. By individuality he means the spiritual perfection that is yet to be.

b. The function of schools, accordingly, is to discover what is the intrinsic worth (potentiality) of the pupils. It is responsible to bring out what is the best among the pupils in body, mind and spirit. The State through schools is required to provide the most congenial environment to the child, to unfold himself freely.

c. The child must feel free to act and to think. Activity is physical as well as mental. Through free mental activity individuality can be developed most desirably. The individuality of the learner has to be respected. His needs, interests and purposes have to be given due recognition and satisfaction.

MAIN CRITICISM OF THE INDIVIDUAL AIMS OF EDUCATION

The exaggerated claim of the individual may have an adverse effect on the collective welfare of the society. *An individual cannot be conceived in isolation from society.*

SOCIAL AIM OF EDUCATION

Several educators and others are of the view that social development of the individual is the aim of education. An individual is a member of the society and he must learn to adjust himself to the needs and aspirations of the society. There are situations when individuals have to sacrifice their individual interests for the greater good of the society.

The social aim in the simple form stresses that society is necessary for the individual to develop. According to them an "*isolated individual is a figment of imagination.*"

When society is considered more than a group of individuals, when its organization is so compact that there exists an idealized metaphysical entry over and above the individual citizen, it transcends all the desires and aspirations of the individual. The sole aim of education then becomes the good of the society.

A CRITICAL EVALUATION OF THE SOCIAL AIMS OF EDUCATION

a. There is every possibility that the social aim of education may be misused and misinterpreted. In its extreme application, it may lead to dangerous consequences.
b. A totalitarian society uses all the media of educating the masses. The individual loses his importance as a person. He occupies a position similar to a cog in the wheel. The State becomes omnipotent.
c. The lives and destinies of people are shaped according to the needs of the society. The individual is so developed that he is required to help in the progress and prosperity of the society only. Schools are State-controlled. Curriculum is planned, constructed and organized by the State to serve its own interest.
d. The methods of instruction are determined by the State. No individual is permitted to have his own claims.
e. Sparta was such a totalitarian State which emphasized the good of society at the expense of the good of the individual. Each individual was born not for himself, but, for the State.
f. The country imparted military training to all its citizens so that it could defend itself from the enemies who surrounded it from all sides. Moral training was given through repressive measures.
g. Discipline was brutal. Punishment was frequent.
h. Nazi Germany was another such State which believed in its own absolute power. The whole educational system, from the primary to the university level, was rigidly controlled. Individuality was crushed.

ASPECTS OF SOCIAL AIM IN THE LIBERAL FORM

a. Democratic countries like India, England and America believe in the good of the society. They try to achieve it through education for citizenship and education for social service.
b. **John Dewey** interprets social aim of education a bit differently. He says that the aim of education is to make an individually socially efficient by unfolding the potentialities of an individual in social pursuits.

SYNTHESIS OF INDIVIDUAL AND SOCIAL AIMS

a. We have two kind of States-democratic and socialistic-idealistic. In the democratic set up we can hope to achieve a synthesis of education for individuality and education for the preservation of the State. But, such a reconciliation is not possible in a totalitarian State.

b. We cannot strike balance between two aims of education, social and individual in a State like Sparta and Nazi Germany.

c. A democratic State uses education as an instrument for its own promotion and preservation, as a totalitarian State does. Both types of States maintain that there is a conflict between one's individual desires and one's duties as a citizen. The democratic State, unlike the other one, requires that the individual should put the needs and desires of others before his own.

d. The different shows to be fallacious. No education can be technical if it is not liberal and no education can be liberal unless it is technical. There is no education which does not impart both technique and intellectual vision.

e. The modern trend, therefore, is to consider general and technical education as complementary. It is now considered necessary to give a course of liberal education first and then to offer vocational or technical education.

f. In the earlier stages general education with vocational bias may be given and purely vocational or technical education may be postponed for later ones.

g. In the traditional society there was an antithesis between liberal and vocational education. The upper class was considered to be fit for education and the lower class required performing work in the field, in the factory and in the mines.

We may sum up the discussion with the views of Jawaharlal Nehru.

"Education has mainly two aspects, the cultural aspect which makes a person grow and the productive aspect which makes a person do things. Both are essential. Everybody should be a producer as well as a good citizen and not a sponge on another person even though the other person may be one's own husband or wife."

TYPES OF EDUCATION

Broadly speaking, education is of three types i.e., formal, non-formal and informal education.

FORMAL EDUCATION

This type of education is imparted in a school or college. It is consciously and deliberately planned to bring about specific and special influences in the educant. Hence, it is synonymous with educational institutions. School is thus a formal agency of education.

NON-FORMAL EDUCATION

Non-formal education is an arrangement wherein flexibility is the key word. The system is an open one with regard to various aspects of education, i.e. admissions, curricular, place of instruction, mode of instruction and the time and duration of courses are the various examples of such a system.

INFORMAL EDUCATION

Informal education takes into its orbit all indirect influences of the home and the society. The press, the libraries, the films and other such agencies are included as agencies of informal education. Their influences is subtle and imperceptible but at the same time very important and significant.

A COMPARISON OF FORMAL AND INFORMAL EDUCATION

S. No.	Formal Education	Informal Education
1.	It is planned keeping in view some definite aim	It has no definite aims and objectives
2.	It is imparted through formal lesson or well planned means	It is not imparted through any formal lesson or well planned means
3.	There is a ultimate course to be covered during a definite period	There is no such definite course and period
4.	Both the teacher and the taught are alert of the process through which education is imparted	They are not conscious of the process
5.	It is organized by some agency	No organized agency is behind this process
6.	It begins and ends at a particular stage	It is a life-long process. It has no start and no end.
7.	It gives strain of various kinds on the teacher and the taught.	It is natural and hence it does not anybody.

MORAL AIMS AND OBJECTIVES OF EDUCATION

a. Morality is a virtue which includes fellow-feeling, sincerity, justice, honesty, morality, tolerance, self-control, freedom and temperance etc. **According to Herbert**, "*Moral education consists in the suppression of the lower and the primitive impulses and the cultivation of higher ideals.*"

b. Modern educationists are of the view that moral aim should be kept in the forefront and all other educational aims should be subordinated to it. Here, teachers should be made responsible to impart moral education to children.

c. **The Secondary Education Commission says that,** *"we are convinced that it is the business of the school to train individuals who will not only be duly appreciative of their culture and the good qualities of national character and national traditions but will also be able to analyses and evaluate it critically."*

d. It should be stated that moral aim of education has certain limitations also, such as—(a) It neglects many other aspects of personality. (b) It is very difficult to make a distinction between right and wrong. So, morality should never be interpreted as a mere communication of knowledge about morals but it should be interpreted from a wider angle.

SPIRITUAL AIMS AND OBJECTIVES OF EDUCATIONS

The people of the whole world are able to live in peace when they adopt an all-inclusive view of religion and spirituality. The peoples as well as the nations of the world at present have recognized the fundamentals of universal human rights that they should acknowledge and celebrate the oneness of all the world's religions.

In our country from the time of Upanishadic Age up to the modern times, the saints, sages and different philosophers from Lord Krishna to Rishi Aurobinda Ghose, and also others, have kept the lamp of our religion as well as spiritualism burning. It is through introspection, intuition and the Yoga of self-restraint; the Indian philosophers have realized and confirmed the existence of soul as the centre of all activities (such as will and force). Material world is nothing but the subservient to soul.

Spiritualism has at present penetrated deeply into every corner of human and social life of Indian culture. Even, there is at present growing consciousness in the West about spiritualism.

The present world has come to the conclusion that there is something beyond this physical world that governs us.

There is a growing consciousness even in the West about the spiritual values of life. But, the major responsibility of accelerating it for peace mainly falls upon our Nation. So, in such a critical context, as an Indian it is needed for us not only to preserve but also to spread our traditional spiritual heritage and ideals in the whole world. Our present educational plans and programmes must have its ultimate aim to develop the spiritual qualities. Because absence of spiritual education has resulted destruction, aggression, hatred, exploitation, selfishness etc.

Each and every lesson of spiritual education must ensure children's intellectual, emotional as well as spiritual aspect of life. The approach of each lesson must follow three parts.

These are :

a. Direct use of the Sacred Writings of the World's religious traditions (i.e. the Lord's Prayer, Proverbs, Verses from the Gita, Koran etc.).

b. To relate learning activities to deepen understanding about various aspects of spiritualism.

c. To explain different stories or Sacred Passages to deepen perception and encourage students for bold expression.

CULTURAL AIM AND OBJECTIVE OF EDUCATION

a. Cultural aim of education means to cultures the individual. The word **"culture"** is interpreted differently in different countries from time to time. Sometimes it is explained in terms of ways of living, varieties of entertainment, general behaviour and standard of fine arts in society.

b. It is also explained in relation with love of music, dancing, literature and refined social behaviour. Some consider it as smoking, drinking, gambling etc. Cultural goal of education gives emphasis on developments of noble ideas, attitudes and pattern of behaviour.

THE HIGHLIGHTING MERITS OR STANDPOINTS OF CULTURAL AIM OF EDUCATION ARE AS FOLLOWS

a. Cultural aim of education helps to modify the innate tendencies of a child which are originally animal nature.

b. Culture helps an individual to have harmonious development with the environment.

c. A cultured person gives up selfishness and narrow ideas from his mind and devote himself to the service of high ideals.

d. Cultural aim trains an individual to spend his leisure time profitably.

THERE ARE ALSO SOME SHORTCOMINGS OF THIS AIM : THESE ARE –

a. The supporters of this aim emphasize only the glory of the past events but an individual cannot live properly only depending on the past.

b. This object has failed to solve his livelihood problems.

c. The society cannot develop only depending upon dancing, singing, gambling, painting etc.

d. This aim has its limitation to bring all round personality progress of child.

Hence, cultural aim of education can't be accepted as the sole aim of education.

4

Development of Secondary Education in India

HISTORY

The history of the development of secondary education in India begins from the days British introduced their system of education. The East India Company was established in 1599 but, the year from which it started ruling the country was 1765 and from this year onwards it began to take interest in drawing out educational policies for this country. In 1813, East India Company was asked to take responsibility of education of Indians by the British Parliament and one lakh of rupees per annum were set apart for this. This amount was raised to ten lakhs in 1833.

WOOD'S DESPATCH

The Wood's Despatch of 1854 was an important landmark in the development of educational policy in this country. This despatch laid the foundation for the establishment of universities and gave a direction and purpose to school education.

The proper emphasis to secondary education and its emergence as a district stage of education can be traced to Hunter Commission of 1882. This commission was appointed to review the functioning of the programmes and principles of Wood's Despatch and to recommend such measures which were needed to make functional that policy which had been propagated by Wood's Despatch and which in the opinion of the commission were desirable.

HUNTER COMMISSION

According to Hunter Commission, Secondary Education was that education which was given to the children between the ages of 12 and 18. But this commission envisaged that secondary education stage is merely the preparatory stage for higher education. This was not a very progressive view but Hunter Commission recommendation could be considered as the first time recognition of secondary education stage.

Macauley's Minutes which were an important landmark in the history of Indian education emphasized the adoption of English system of education. Macauley recommended that through the teaching of English such a class of Indians be produced which would be Indian in blood and colour but in its attitudes, thinking and behaviour and intellect be English. Keeping this objective in mind the missionaries established secondary schools.

The Wood's Despatch recommended for allocation of more funds for giving grant-in-aid to privately run institution so as to encourage them for providing better education. It also recommended for the adoption of native language as the medium of instruction along with English at the primary and middle stages of education. As a result of its Vernacular Middle schools were opened since in High schools English Medium continued to dominate there were only Anglo-Vernacular school.

Many Committees and Commissions appointed by the government pointedly drew attention to these drawbacks but unfortunately not many concrete steps were taken to remedy the situation. Prominent among such committees etc. were Sadler Commission (1917), Hartog Committee (1929), Wood-Abbot Report (1936-37) and Sargent Plan (1944). An idea of expansion of secondary education can be had from the following figures. In 1916-17, there were 9,24,770 students studying in 4,883 secondary school. In 1922, the number of secondary schools increased to 7,530 in which 11,06,803 students were enrolled. Just before independence in 1946-47 the number of secondary schools was 12,693 and the students enrolled in VI to XI classes were 29,53,995.

It may be noted that even though the expenditure in terms of gross amount in crores went on increasing from plan to plan the percentage of expenditure on secondary education showed little variance, particularly in 5th, 6th and 7th plans.

LADDERS GIVEN BY SECONDARY EDUCATION COMMISSION (1952-53) AND KOTHARI COMMISSION BACKGROUND

a. The word ladder means the division or classification of educational institutions according to standards.

b. The standards start from pre primary to university and each stage help to prepare the next higher stage.

c. It helps to ensure smooth migration of the student from one state to another state.

d. In real sense, the educational ladder in a systematic form was first introduced in India by Wood's Despatch in 1954, which consisted of four stages—the primary, the middle, the high school and the university stage.

EDUCATIONAL LADDRER AS GIVEN BY SECONDARY EDUCATION COMMISSION (1952-53)

The landmark in the reconstruction of India's educational ladder is Secondary Education Commission Report, 1952-53.

a. The first stage of Educational Ladder should be pre-primary or nursery education for 3 years duration. The admission age should be 3 years and the course should be continued up to the age of 6.

b. The next stage of Educational Ladder should be Primary or Junior basis for 4 or 5 years duration.

c. The third stage of ladder is Secondary Education which should be divided into two stages— (a) The Middle or Junior Secondary or Senior Basic stage and should cover a period of 3 years. (b) The Higher Secondary stage, which is the next stage of secondary education and should cover a period of 4 years (from class IX to XII).

d. The fourth stage of ladder is of 3 years' duration (first) Degree course.

The most significant change during the decade that followed the publication of the Mudaliar Commission was the upgrading of high schools in accordance with Higher Secondary pattern. The other significant change that occurred was the introduction of 3 year first degree course.

EDUCATIONAL LADDER SUGGESTED BY KOTHARI COMMISISON

Educational Ladder suggested by Kothari Commission or Indian suggested Commission (1964-66)

a. The educational ladder suggested by the Education Commission was rather flexible but it consisted of 10 years of general school education, 2 years of higher secondary education (general as well as vocational), 3 years of higher education leading to the first degree.

b. The total duration of school education plus university education leading to the first degree as recommended was 15 years, but there was flexibility in the educational ladder.

c. The educational ladder as suggested by the Education Commission of (1964-66) indicates that the system of education (10+2+3) was different from the educational ladder as suggested by the Secondary Education Commission (1952-53) or Mudaliar Commission. Under the latter pattern we had 5 years of lower primary, 3 years of higher primary (or lower secondary), 3 years of higher secondary and 3 years for the first degree in Arts and Sciences. The total duration of school and college education up to the first degree had been 14 years but under the Commission's scheme it was 15 years.

Kothari Commission (1964-66) favoured the lengthening of the duration of schooling by one year, because the longer the duration, the better is the quality of education. It was a popular belief that "*the total period of the educational course and the duration of its different stages have a direct hearing on the quality of education imparted.*"

RECOMMENDATIONS MADE BY SECONDARY EDUCATION COMMISSION (1952-53)

Post-Independence Reconstruction of Education is an important landmark in the history of education in India. Prior to the publication of the report of the Mudaliar Commission, a number of opinions had been expressed for the improvement of secondary education in the country. In real sense the Mudaliar Commissions (1952-53) was the first Commission whose recommendations in this regard were heard and implemented by the Government in the decades.

RECOMMENDATIONS OF THE MUDALIAR COMMISSION

The Mudaliar Commission made a general survey of the entire field of secondary education. It defined the growing needs of the newborn nation. It realized the importance of secondary education in the growth of the country and made the following recommendations : (1) The diversification of courses to suit the tastes and interests of the individual pupils, (2) the introduction of agricultural education, (3) the improvement of scales and status of the teaching community, (4) the national pattern of secondary education, and (5) the introduction of guidance and counseling in schools.

The stated recommendations brought a great change in the nature of secondary education of our country. Two Programmes that were carried in a planned way throughout the country was—(a) conversion of high schools to higher secondary ones, and (b) establishment of multipurpose schools. Moreover, special measures were taken to improve the lot of teachers the teaching of Science and English in secondary school.

RECOMMENDATIONS MADE BY KOTHARI COMMISSION

The Education Commission (1964-66) was appointed by the Government of India in July 1964 to advice on the national pattern of education and on the general principles and policies of development of education at all stages and in all aspects. The Commission was headed by Prof. D. S. Kothari, Chairman of University Grants Commission and the report of the Commission is, therefore, called, the **"Kothari Commission Report"**. The Commission submitted its report in 1966. The report is a voluminous one and contained a detailed analysis of all the aspects of education at various stages.

VARIEGATED RECOMMENDATIONS MADE BY THE COMMISSION (1964-66)

Fourfold goals of Education. The Commission suggested the following :

1. To increase productivity.
2. To achieve national integration.
3. To accelerate the process of modernization.
4. To cultivate social, moral and spiritual values.

a. Stress on Science Education. Science and Mathematics must become an integral part of school education and taught on a compulsory basis to all pupils during the first ten years of schooling.

b. Every primary school should have a science corner or a room to keep specimens, models and charts with the necessary storage facilities. A minimum of one laboratory-cum-lecture room should be provided in every higher primary school.

c. Vocationalization is another vital programme which can bring education into closer relationship with productivity is to give a strong vocational bias to secondary education and to increase the emphasis on agricultural and technological education at the university stage.

d. Common School System. A common school system of public education should be introduced.
e. Ten Years of Schooling of General Education. The first ten years of schooling should cover a primary stage of seven or eight years and a lower secondary stage of three or two years providing a course of general education without any specialization.
f. Two years duration of Higher Secondary Stage. The Higher Secondary Stage should be extended to cover a period of two years and to be located exclusively in schools.
g. Instructional Days in Schools. The number of instructional days in a year should be increased to about 234 (or 39 weeks) for schools and 216 (36 weeks) for colleges and pre-primary schools.
h. Maximum Utilization of School Facilities : The libraries, laboratories, workshops, crafts heads etc. should be opened all the year round and should be utilized for at least eight hours a day.
i. College to be related to a Number of Schools. Each college can be functionally related to a number of secondary schools in the neighborhood and enabled to provide extension services and guidance to them to improve their standards.
j. Free Textbooks at the Primary Stage. At the primary stage a programme of providing free textbooks should be given very high priority and introduced immediately.
k. Book Banks in Schools. A programme of books banks should be introduced in secondary schools and in institutions of higher education.
l. Adequate No. of Scholarships. The top 10 per cent of the students in educational institutions should be given small grants annually for the purchase of books which need not necessarily be textbooks.

AREAS OF NATIONAL POLICY ON EDUCATION (1986)

BACKGROUND

With the attainment of independence there has been a demand for changing our educational system. From time to time various Commissions have proposed their educational policy from their own viewpoint. The National Policy of 1986 marked a significance change in the history of education in post-Independence India. It laid stress on the need for a radical reconstruction of the education system of the country.

NEW EDUCATION POLICY

In January 1985, the Government of India announced that a New Education Policy would be formulated for the Country. The major areas of National Policy of Education (N.P.E) 1986 may be mentioned in the following way:

1. Important role of Education
2. Establishment of a National System of Education
3. Problem of Centre-State Partnership in Education
4. Education for Equality

5. Universalization of Elementary Education
6. Promotion of Adult Education
7. Pace-setting Schools
8. Vocationalization of Education
9. Delinking Degrees from Jobs
10. Raising the status of teachers
11. Technical and management of education
12. Resource mobilization

1. IMPORTANT ROLE OF EDUCATION

Education is considered as essential for all. It is fundamental for our all-around development of material as well as spiritual aspects of life. It is essential investment of present as well as future. It helps to develop manpower for different levels of economy of the nation.

2. ESTABLISHMENT OF A NATIONAL SYSTEM OF EDUCATION

a. The concept of a National System of Education implies that up to a given level, all students, irrespective of caste, creed, location, or sex, have access to education of a comparable quality. To achieve this the Government will initiate appropriately funded programmes.
b. The National System of Education envisages a common educational structure. The **10+2+3** structure has now been accepted in all parts of the country. Regarding the further break-up of the first 10 years efforts will be made to move towards an elementary system comprising 5 years of primary education and 3 years of upper primary, followed by 2 years of High School.
c. The National System of Education will be based on a National curricular framework which contains a common core along with other components that are flexible.
d. To promote equality, it will be necessary to provide for equal opportunity to all not only in access, but also in the conditions for success.
e. Minimum levels of learning will be laid down for each stage of education. Steps will be taken to foster among students an understanding of the diverse cultural and social systems of the people living in different parts of the country.
f. Other institutions which will be strengthened to play an important role in giving shape to the National System of Education are the University Grants Commission, the All India Council of Technical Education, The Indian Council of Agricultural Research and The Indian Medical Council.
g. These institutions together with National Council of Educational Research and Training and National Institute of Educational Planning and Administration, will be involved in implementing the Education Policy.

3. PROBLEM OF CENTRE-STATE PARTNERSHIP IN EDUCATION

The Constitutional Amendment of 1976, which includes Education in the concurrent list, was a far-reaching step whose implications—substantive, financial and administrative—require a new sharing of responsibility between the Union Government and the States in respect of vital area of national life.

4. EDUCATION AND EQUALITY

The NPE of 1986 will give special emphasis on the removal of disparities and to equalize educational opportunity by attending to the specific needs of those who have been denied equality so far. Education should be considered as an agent of change of the status of woman.

5. UNIVERSALIZATION OF ELEMENTARY EDUCATION

The New Policy will lay special emphasis on elementary education and emphasizes on two aspects–

a. Universal enrollment and Universal retention of children up to 14 years of age, and
b. A Substantial improvement in the quality of education.

All the necessary steps will be taken to ensure that the quality of non-formal education is comparable with formal education.

A phased drive, symbolically called Operation Blackboard will be undertaken with immediate effect to improve primary schools all over the country.

6. PROMOTION OF ADULT EDUCATION

The whole nation must take bold steps to the eradication of illiteracy, particularly in the age-group of 15 to 35. The Central and State Governments, political parties and their mass organizations, the mass media and educational institutions must commit themselves to mass literacy programmes of diverse nature.

7. PACE-SETTING SCHOOLS

In the **NPE** the Pace-setting schools or Navodaya Vidyalayas are meant for children with special talent or aptitude. It is universally accepted that children with special talent should be provided opportunities to proceed at a faster pace, by making good quality education available to them, irrespective of their capacity to pay for it.

8. VOCATIONALIZATION OF EDUCATION

The introduction of vocational education is crucial in **NPE (1986)**. Such courses are specially meant to enhance individual employability, to reduce the mismatch between the demand and supply of skilled manpower, and to provide an alternative for those who are pursuing higher education without particular interest or purpose.

9. DELINKING DEGREES FROM JOBS

The National Policy on Education visualize delinking of University degrees from the requirement for recruitment to services for which a University degree need not be a necessary qualification.

10. TECHNICAL AND MANAGEMENT OF EDUCATION

In the New Education Policy of 1986, technical and management of education is one of the more significant components of Human Resource Development spectrum with great potential for adding value to products and services and for contributing to the national economy and improving quality of life of the people.

11. RESOURCE MOBILIZATION

Resources will be raised by mobilizing donations to maintain school buildings and supplies of some consumable, raising fees at the higher levels of education and affecting some savings by the efficient use of facilities.

10+2+3 SYSTEM OF EDUCATION, ITS FEATURES AND PROBLEMS

Restructuring the educational pattern is one of the novel experiments in the field of our modern education. The New Structural Pattern of Education (**10+2+3**) was proposed by the Education Commission (**1964-66**) for the introduction of a uniform educational structure all over the country.

THE NEW PATTERN OF EDUCATION

The new pattern of education, which is commonly known as **10+2+3** pattern, has been evolved after a lot of discussions and deliberations in various Committees and commissions. The various steps of this new pattern of education are

a. The first stage covers ten years of schooling for all for imparting general education, with emphasis on Science and Mathematics, and the addition of new subjects like Work-Experience, Physical Education and Aesthetic Activities.

b. The second stage, which is of 2 years duration, provides diversified and specialized courses with more emphasis on Vocationalization. During this stage an attempt will be made to identify the individual differences such as learners ability of physical, intellectual emotional etc.

c. The third stage, i.e. +3 stage is the college course of three years duration, leading to first Degree of B.A./B.Sc.

HIGHLIGHTING FEATURES OF 10+2+3 PATTERN OF EDUCATION

THE NEW PATTERN OF EDUCATION POSSESSES THE FOLLOWING FEATURES

a. It helps to develop the scientific attitude and interests among the students.

b. The pattern maintains uniformity of educational system all over the country.

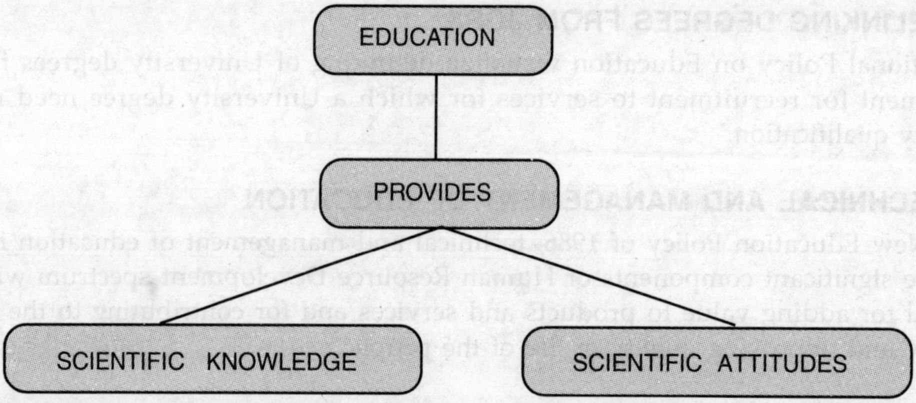

Fig. 6. Education – Its Pivotal Role

c. The New Pattern of Education is suitable for higher stage of learning.
d. It helps to develop the sense of National Integration in the mind of the students.
e. It encourages vocational courses and trains the learners to love for manual work.
f. It helps to check the heavy rush towards higher education.
g. It suggests for the introduction of diversification of courses.

CONCLUSION

The New Pattern was launched in the country, but the expectations were not fulfilled. Different states did not even accept the proposal. Those who accepted the proposal left the idea.

Those that accepted the idea and tried to convert their higher schools to higher secondary ones did so only to gain central assistance. The effect was that in place uniformity there came diversity.

5

Education and Citizenship

TRAINING IN CITIZENSHIP AS AN GOAL OF EDUCATION

Today, variegated countries are wedded to democracy. Democracy is not a way of Government, it is more than that; a way of life. The better success of the democracy depends upon proper training of citizen. Education has to equip the young boys and girls for it. Education for citizenship is, hence a vital aim of education.

EDUCATION FOR CITIZENSHIP AS ENUNCIATED BY UNITED STATES OF AMERICA

United States of America is supposed to be the most successful and greatest democracy of world today. It trains its children for citizenship. Really speaking, U.S.A. was the first country to chalk out a plan education for citizenship. Training of youngmen for democracy is the real goal of education there. These aims have been incorporated in the statement of Policies Commission of United States of America.

VOCATIONAL ADJUSTMENT

There are a lot of problems in the life of an individual. Among these problems, the problem of adjustment in various aspects of life is very important. Some educationists are of the view that the problem of vocational adjustment is the most important problem in the life of an individual. In educational arena, this problem must be treated as an important one, and some creative steps must be taken by the teachers enable children to cultivate such capacity as they may solve their vocational problems.

WHY VOCATIONAL EDUCATION IS SO NECESSARY

The educationists have advanced the following reasons, which clearly justify the need for vocational education:

a. Vocation education enables an individual to earn his livelihood comfortably. He grows self-sufficient and self-existent. He is not more a parasite or a drag on the society.

b. It brings about national prosperity and also brings about advancement of the society.
c. The vocational adjustment leads to all other adjustments like social adjustment, leisure and moral adjustment etc. Morality and culture grow where is proper vocational adjustment.
d. An economically self-sufficient person helps the country in its economic, political and social developments.

PROVISION FOR VOCATIONAL GUIDANCE

In order to achieve the objective of vocational adjustment, the provision for vocational guidance has been made. According to the interests, nature and aptitudes of the children, they are guided by the guidance workers.

6

Aims of Education in India

IMPORTANCE OF AIMS OF EDUCATION IN INDIA

Every country has to have certain goals of education. These aims are to be in conformity with the aims of the society and national objectives. This is true about India as well.

India is known for its education, variegated culture and philosophy. Indian civilization is one of the oldest civilization in the world. India has embraced all the culture in itself.

AIMS OF EDUCATION IN INDIA IN DIFFERENT AGES

History of Education in India may be divided into the following four heads :

a. Vedic and Brahmanic age;
b. Buddhist age;
c. Medieval age; and
d. Modern Democratic age

AIMS OF EDUCATION IN VEDIC AND BRAHMANIC AGE

During this period following were the aims of education:

a. Close between education and leisure.
b. Spiritual development.
c. Acquisition of knowledge.
d. Character building.
e. Development of personality.
f. Development of culture.
g. Development of social element.

AIMS OF EDUCATION DURING BUDDHIST PERIOD

Buddhist period brought about some change in outlook towards life and this was reflected in the education.

AIMS OF EDUCATION IN MEDIAEVAL PERIOD

This was basically the Islamic period. Muslim rulers dominated the political as well as social scene. The education of this period was based on the tenets of Islam.

AIMS OF EDUCATION IN DEMOCRATIC INDIA

Since India has been emancipated from slavery. It has decided to live in democratic way. Ours is a secular democratic State and hence education in the birth right of all.

7

Society and Education

EDUCATION STANDS FOR

Education is, in fact, 'learning through experiences'. Pestalozzi has remarked that education is "a natural, harmonious and progressive development of man's innate powers".

John Dewey has defined it as "the development of all those capacities in the individual which will enable him to control his environment and fulfil his responsibilities". Hence, education is a life long process.

WHAT IS SOCIETY?

It is an old saying that man is a social animal. Outside society man does not have any important status. We carry on communication and exchange in the society. Man has to have relations with his fellow-beings. Such a situation connects him into society.

Society is nothing but a group of such individuals who live within a geographical area and bound together by certain common experience and cultural ideals.

RELATIONSHIP BETWEEN THE SOCIETY AND THE EDUCATION

If one hand man is influenced by the society, on the other he influences the society as well. Every group of individuals, when organized, lays down certain goals and ideologies. Every member of the society is bound by those goals and aims. This binding takes place through a process of change in the individual which is nothing but education. It is the society that has established institutions to educate the members of the society.

INFLUENCE OF SOCIETY ON EDUCATION

Society also shows a lot of influence on education. People go to schools for the fulfilment of their needs and requirements. The schools have to gear up their training in accordance with the requirements of the society. In the words of John Dewey, "School should be true representative of the society".

In the absence of such a gearing up the education may have a value in itself but it can have no importance for the society. Society influence the education and the schools very much. Schools have to provide for an education which will be useful for the fulfilment of the requirements and objectives of the society. In the present scenario, socialization of the schools is taking place at a very rapid. This is all due to this relationship.

HOW DOES EDUCATION INFLUENCE SOCIETY

In brief, education affects society in the following ways:

a. Education helps the presentation of culture and the values of the society.
b. Society is developed through education because the sense of sociability is created by it.
c. Education controls the society and maintains discipline in it. The defects and the bad influences that might creep into the society are checked by education. It eradicates social evils and bad traditions.
d. Education prepares good citizens. It is the education which makes us conscious of our duties and responsibilities.

IMPACT OF SOCIETY ON EDUCATION

Really, society leaves its effect on education in the following manners:

a. Different aims of the societies are achieved through education. Education takes its shape in accordance with the end of the society.
b. The system of education is apt to change when the events of social life are changed and it is changed according to the needs of the society.

8

Social Change and School

SOCIAL CHANGE–A REALITY

Social change is a reality. It is a part and parcel of society. Variegated factors are accountable for its occurrence. Social changes are brought about sometimes by individuals and sometimes certain events. The life of a man and that of the society as a whole undergoes the methods of change regularly.

TERM OF THE SOCIAL CHANGE

Scholars like Herbart Spencer who believe in biological concept of change, think that the social evolution and social change are synonymous. Spencer viewed that social change is gradual, uniform and progressive and it goes ahead "from less satisfactory to more satisfactory adjustments." In this biological causes are fully responsible.

DEFINITIONS OF SOCIAL CHANGE

The two important definitions of social changes are as under:

1. According to MacIver, "Social change is a process responsive to many types of changes, to changes in the man-made condition of living, to changes in the attitude of the man and changes that go beyond human control to the biological and physical nature".
2. In the words of Delbert C. Miller, "Social change refers to a pattern of social relationship in a given social setting, which exhibits change over some definite period of time".

FORM OF SOCIAL CHANGE

Social change indicates itself in the following forms and aspects of the society:

a. Political changes which cover changes in the political power and the administration of the entire State.

b. Economic changes that cover changes in industry, agriculture, business, trade and other allied agencies.
c. Moral changes – Moral changes are those that bring about changes in the moral ideas, religion and religious principles and other factors.
d. Religious changes impact changes in different religious institutions like church, congregation, religious sects.
e. Scientific changes are caused by new inventions which have their own influence on the life and the philosophy of the society.

FACTORS ACCOUNTABLE FOR THE SOCIAL CHANGES

There are variegated factors that bring about social changes. These factors may be studied briefly under the following heads:

PHYSICAL ENVIRONMENT

The environment or the nature continues to change and this change brings about a lot of change in the entire society and its life.

BIOLOGICAL FACTORS

MacIver and Page have correctly viewed that biological factors change and prepare the way for social change. These factors come from generation to generation.

TECHNOLOGICAL FACTOR

Many of the sociologists have laid great impact on the technological factor. They say that this is a very vital factor in the social change.

CULTURAL FACTOR

Culture is really, based on society. People belonging to one group of culture have philosophy of life of their own. This philosophy is different from the philosophy of other group.

EDUCATION AS A FACTOR IN SOCIAL CHANGE

Over and above the factors and reasons enumerated in the preceding lines, education is a pivotal factor responsible for social change. It is the education that brings about the assimilation of the cultural norms and expands it from generation to generation.

ROLE OF THE SCHOOL IN SOCIAL CHANGE

Education is a source for the preparation of life. It equips the individuals to be able to face life. In the society, every individual has to undertake creative activities not only for himself and his family but for the entire society too. Such an activity, when backed by education, has a great value and norms. In this arena the following quotation is very pertinent:

"Education is a preparation for life. It has to train the individual for leading a successful life in the world in which he is placed. The world in which he has to live is not a static world; it is constantly changing. He comes to live in a culture in which changes are taking place at every moment and still more momentous changes may take place in the future. Education has to equip him for his ever changing order".

In the conclusion we can say that really social change is a reality. Without it society is not complete. Social change makes the social relationship more stronger.

9

Sociological Tendency in Education

SOCIOLOGICAL INCLINATION IN EDUCATION

When we talk of social development in education we think by it sociological development. Sociological development in education creates such ability in man, through which one succeeds in achieving happiness in social life. There could be a marked close relationship between education and society, because no man can be accomplished without society.

SOCIOLOGY AND EDUCATION

In the arena of social progress, education has a pivotal role to play. Education performs the following functions:

1. Education is the chief agency of imparting knowledge. It nourishes body and mind with fine qualities of personality.
2. Education plays the role of social control. It objects at formation of good conduct and moral behaviour. It teaches discipline.
3. Education protects culture and civilization from age to age.

EDUCATIONAL SOCIOLOGY

In every society whether its form is old or new, there are variegated types of public institutions, committees etc., which fulfil the different types of the individual as well as the society. Requirements connected with livelihood, entertainment, administrative, educational etc. are fulfilled by these institutions.

The subject of education which studies institutions of the society etc., is called 'Educational Sociology'. According to Ottoway, "The education is an activity which goes on in society and its aims and methods depend on the nature of the society on which it takes place".

AIMS OF EDUCATIONAL SOCIOLOGY

George S. Herrington has said the following aims of educational sociology–

1. It aims at knowing the contribution of teacher to society and school to social development. It also studies the different factors affecting school education.
2. To stud0 economic and social points of view in the light of education.
3. To discuss various social factors which affect a man in the society.
4. Socialization of curriculum.
5. To introduce system of research and explanatory thinking for the light of these aims.

EDUCATION AND SOCIALIZATION

Education has always been a source of socialization and social control. By socialization, man becomes fit for social living. In this process family, playgrounds, school, college and religion play an important role. Hence, in the modern era formal and informal agencies of education dominate the society, so far as the socialization is concerned.

Control is a reciprocal act between the society and education. It indicates to the truth that sometimes education controls the society, while sometimes it is the society that controls education.

10

Scientific Tendency in Education

INTRODUCTION

Scientific tendency in education, as it is known today, is basically the contribution of Herbert Spencer to the field of education. In fact, it owes existence to Naturalism. Pestalozzi with his importance on the use of 'sense organs' and 'self-experience' carried it a step ahead.

DEFINITION OF SCIENTIFIC TENDENCY

Since we have from the very beginning started using the words 'scientific tendency' let us make its meaning clear as well. Really speaking, this is 'an ideology in the field of educational arena which gave greater importance to natural sciences in curriculum and other fields of education'. This tendency also led to the prevalence of Inductive method in the field of education.

HIGHLIGHTING CHARACTERISTICS OF SCIENTIFIC TENDENCY

The following are the highlighting characteristics of scientific inclination:

a. In this tendency, emphasis has been laid on inclusion of such subjects in the curriculum as have a direct utility in life.

b. This tendency opposes the literary education.

c. This tendency has given a new thinking to liberal education.

d. This tendency has introduced a new term of education.

e. Since emphasis is laid on teaching of scientific subjects, hence, this education lays stress on Inductive Method of education.

f. This is really a materialistic way of education. It believes that the material world and its laws are true.

11

Psychological Tendency in Education

INTRODUCTION

Before the progress of the psychological inclination in education, the educands were forced to accept the ideals of the teachers, bookish knowledge, burden of the curriculum, repressive discipline etc. No consideration was made to the interests, desires, aptitudes, needs and feelings of the educands.

IMPORTANT FEATURES OF PSYCHOLOGICAL TENDENCY

Following are the chief characteristics of psychological tendency:

a. **Education should be based on Psychology** – According to thinkers and educationists like Rousseau, Pestalozzi, Froebel, Herbart, Plato, Montessori, Draver etc. education should be based on psychology, because it is the study of human behaviour.

b. **Importance of child** – According to the old viewpoint of education, the position of teacher was considered equal to that of God.

c. **Necessity of the study of child** – It is the main duty of the teacher that he should understand the original tendencies, needs, aptitudes and feelings of the children.

d. **To impart education to child considering him as a child** – Since education has been based on psychology, education is imparted to child in accordance with his ability, needs and capacity.

e. **Learning by doing** – According to the new viewpoint of education, learning by doing or activity has assumed much importance.

f. **Importance of play** – In the modern method of education, play occupies a very vital place. According to psychologists and educationists, play is natural and pleasure-giving tendency by birth.

g. **Importance of freedom and discipline** – The importance of freedom and discipline has increased also much in the modern education that scholars have started advocating the "Emancipationist Discipline".

h. **Status of educator as the friend, guide and brother** – According to the old viewpoint of education, the status of educator was equal to God. Children were scared of the teacher.

12

Philosophical Tendency in Education

PHILOSOPHY STANDS FOR

Before analyzing the main theme of this chapter, i.e. the philosophical bases of education it is necessary to be acquainted with the true meaning of the term "Philosophy". There is no unanimity of opinion among the thinkers and philosophers regarding its real meaning and subject matter.

DEFINITION OF PHILOSOPHY

Following definitions of philosophy will help to understand the real meaning of the word philosophy :

1. **Aristotle** defined philosophy as a science which discovers the real nature of supernatural elements or knowledge of what is eternal.
2. **Hegel** defined philosophy as knowledge of supernatural elements or knowledge of what is eternal.
3. **Fichte** defined philosophy as a science of knowledge.
4. According to **Bradley** philosophy is an attempt to know reality as against appearance.

PHILOSOPHY AND EDUCATION

There exists an intimate connection between philosophy and education. Fichte in his "Address to the German people" observed that the art of education would never attain clearness in itself without philosophy. The philosophical views of the outstanding philosophers like Plato, Aristotle, Socrates, Rousseau and others have exerted tremendous impact on the theory and practice. In the words of Sir John Adams "Education is the dynamic side of philosophy".

PHILOSOPHY OF NATURALISM IN EDUCATION

Naturalism is one of the major schools of philosophy. It possesses there distinct forms viz (1) Physical Naturalism (2) Mechanical Naturalism (3) Biological Naturalism. This school of philosophy is not prepared to accept anything beyond nature and other than nature.

In the words of Sir John Adams – "Naturalism is a term loosely applied in education theory to systems of training that are not dependent on schools and looks but on the manipulation of the actual life of the educated".

13

The Role of Teacher

INTRODUCTION

"The teacher is not merely the fountain of facts, the walking encyclopedia and the universal provider of useful information to the young, but their guide, philosopher and friend, the skilled builder of their intellect".

– Wren

In the words of Wren "the teacher is not merely the fountain of facts, the walking encyclopedia and the universal provider of useful information to the young, but their guide, philosopher and friend, the skilled builder of their intellect."

The role of the teacher in moulding the shape of an educational method cannot be overestimated. Because he is not only the source of inspiration to the children placed under his care, but also their friend philosopher and guide.

FUNCTIONS OF A TEACHER

The real functions of a teacher may be conceived from two standpoints – narrow and broad. Narrowly conceived it is the duty of a teacher to teach his pupils certain topics in a specially designed environment. Imparting of a formal instruction is the only function which the teacher has to discharge.

ELIGIBILITY OF A TEACHER

The teacher has a twofold position in the super structure of teaching method, viz. as a person and as an educator. As an educator he is chiefly accountable for giving formal method to children played under his care.

OTHER QUALIFICATIONS

Besides physical qualifications the teacher is expected to possess the following qualification, viz –

Command over subject-matter

An attractive appearance is not enough for a teacher. In order to impact the pupils in the most effective manner and command respect from him, the teacher must be something of a scholar.

Teaching ability

A good teacher is one who can teach successfully and who can make his pupils follow him. He makes the teaching learning method much easier.

Technical efficiency

Besides knowledge of the subject matter a teacher must have technical efficiency. He is the technical indicator.

Capacity to maintain discipline

The teacher is specially entrusted with the task of teaching. Hence, he cannot achieve success in his duty unless he can maintain discipline in his area.

Strength of personality and character

The personality of the teacher is also an important cause. The modern term of the school is that it is a miniature society.

Knowledge of child-psychology

It is said that "school master is one who studies his scholar's nature as they their books." Hence, one of thc essential requisites for a teachings profession is the knowledge of child-psychology.

Sympathy, suggestion and imitation

The teacher must be mentally strong to the fact that children possess the maid tendencies of sympathy, suggestion and imitation. Children are maid tendencies of sympathy, suggestion and imitation. Children are naturally suggestible and imitative.

Sense of humour

A teacher who is stern and dull witted and who is unable to share the joys and sorrows of his students cannot be a real and successful teacher.

Language usage

The teacher must use lucid and easy language in his class. He must have at his command a rich vocabulary and faultless pronunciation. His speech must be faultless and free from stammering.

CONCLUSION

We are well known that the teacher is the pivot upon the whole method of education turns. In order to make the education system effective and easy, every teacher should try to arouse in the children a high sense of social and moral values to develop in them intellectual, honesty and moral.

14

Teaching as a Profession

INTRODUCTION

School and community are two vital forces that contribute towards the development of the whole child. If he is pulled in several directions by home and school, he shall be lost in uncertain currents. Formal and informal, active and passive agencies have to be co-ordinated in such a way that they supplement and correct the work of each other.

Schools are set up by the community to educate its members and therefore they are to satisfy the needs of community. The community wants them to work as a small community within a large community.

Although the modern child-centre education has shifted the focus of its attention from the subject to the child, the place and importance of teachers in modern education have been accepted by all.

How School Influences Community ?

Influence of the school on the community may be enumerated as under –

1. Problems of community can be solved by the school.
2. Culture of the community is modified by the school.
3. Industrial and vocational progress is influenced by the school.
4. Standard of living of community is reflected in school, and school in turn tries to raise the standard of living of the community.
5. School influences the general environment of the community.

Influence of Community on School

1. Needs of community are reflected in the school.
2. Culture and tradition of the community are learn by students in the school.
3. Values and evils of the community also reflect there in the school.

4. Living standard of life of community is reflected there.
5. Programmes and policies are also reflected there in the schools.

Strengthening Interdependence of the School and the Community

Valuable points of suggestions are given below:

1. Each school should have a local advisory committee consisting the nobler persons of the locality. They should advise not to interfere.
2. 'Parents Day' function should be organized every year in the school campus. On such occasion parents should be asked to speak on topics of school-welfare.
3. Adult education classes should be started in the evening hours.
4. In the evening hours, library should be opened for community people.
5. Matches between the members of the school staff and those of the community may be organized to expand the relationship between the two.

CONCLUSION

To sum up in the words of the Secondary Education Commission, "What we should like to see, is a two way of channel so that the problems that arise in the home and community life and the realistic experiences gained should be brought into school so that education may be based on them and be intimately connected with real life, and on the other hand, the new knowledge, skills, attitudes and values acquired in the school should be carried into the home life to solve its problems, to raise standards and link up the teachers, parents and children in one compact and naturally helpful group."

Exactly alike, the teacher has to take individual care and give proper treatment to his students. And for this, he must have a detailed knowledge on the students individual aptitudes, their physical, mental and temperamental requirements.

15

Curriculum

INTRODUCTION

A curriculum, according to dictionary meaning, is the track of a race course through which the race horse reaches its target. In education, curriculum means the course of studies through which a pupil would traverse in order to attain his aim.

Curriculum is a very important factor in education. It changes according to the situations and the circumstances of any country. The curriculum of education is decided in accordance with the policies and programmes of the nation. Curriculum generally denotes all those tasks that are performed by school students.

Definition of Curriculum

Different authors have given different definitions. Some base the definition on its narrow sense whiles others define it its broad sense, here, we are giving some important definitions on curriculum.

1. According to Cunninghum, "It (Curriculum) is a toll in the hands of the artist (teacher) to mould his material (pupil) according to this ideal (Objective) in his studio (school)".
2. In the words of Froebel, "Curriculum should be conceived as an epitome of the rouged whole of the knowledge and experience of the human race".

The Phases of the Curriculum

School children come from different phase of life. Some of them belong to rural and some come from urban areas. Hence, they differ on account of their background. Keeping these facts in view, the curriculum should be so framed, that it may adjust every section of students. This will enable the students to school their path of life.

At the primary step, students are generally between 6 to 11 years of age and at the secondary step, students are from 12 to 14 years. The needs of both the groups of students are more or less the same. In short, they are –

(a) Sports (b) Acquaintance with the laws of health and hygiene (c) Knowledge of worldly atmosphere and social life. (d) Exchange of their new experiences with their friends and senior. (e) The fulfilments of instincts of imitation, construction and sociability.

AIMS AND OBJECTS OF A SCHOOL CURRICULUM

The curriculum aims at developing a well-organized personality of the child so as to enable him to adjust himself and to improve his social and physical environment in active co-operation with others. In short, the following are the aims and objectives that should be kept in view while making school curriculum –

a. To cultivate, exert and inspire the full progress of the child.
b. To stimulate the students to think, to development of the child.
c. To develop the traits of their character – honesty, judgement, co-operation, friendliness and goodwill.
d. To promote a better human relationship.
e. To intimate the students with the humanities, the arts, the natural and social sciences and religion.
f. To create democratic sense citizenship.
g. To cultivate a lively civic sense by increasing the social, economic and political understanding of the individuals and by increasing their loyalty to democracy.

Lastly, we can say that curriculum is the essential and important factor in educational process. Since education involves the life itself and its experiences aides by external knowledge, the curriculum may be defined as the aggregate of subject matters, activities and experiences cultured and gained by the pupil in his school life. It is an epitome of the rounded whole of the knowledge of the human race.

16

Evaluation

CONCEPT OF EVALUATION

Evaluation is the measurement of the student's development towards significant goods of education. It is a method of appraising the students achievement. Writing Stone says that "Evaluation is a relatively new technical term introduced to designate a more comprehensive concept of measurement than is implied in conventional tests and measurement."

Evaluation measures changes in a desired direction. Evaluation is the device which provides evidence regarding the development of students towards educational objectives.

SCOPE OF EVALUATION

It may be evident from the scope of evaluation is much wider than the scope of measurement. We may consider the following points regarding the scope of evaluation:

1. The evaluation is concerned not only with the appraisal of achievement but also with its improvement.
2. The evaluation has also the diagnostic function to perform. Through it the weaknesses or deficiencies of students are diagnosed and remedial measures taken.
3. Evaluation is inevitable. Every educational or social programme is initiated, continued or discarded because of some form of evaluation.
4. Evaluation extends to all steps and levels of education.
5. The scope of evaluation is also extended to the development of abilities in the learner for self-appraisal. The learners may become competent evaluators of their own goals, experiences and accomplishments.

SIGNIFICANCE OF EVALUATION

The significance of evaluation in educational process may be explained as follows:

These are with reference to the planning and implementation of an educational programme.

a. Through evaluation we may identify and examine the values inherent in the educational programme, policy or process.
b. Evaluation can lead to the formulation or clarifying the objectives, goals, purposes of the educational programme.
c. Evaluation gives the criteria for measuring success.
d. Evaluation determines and explains the extent of success and failure.
e. It can determine the effect of the educational programme.
f. It can lead to the recommending of the alteration, replacement or discontinuance of the programme.
g. It can lead to the assessment of the norm, benefit or social utility of the programme.

CONTINUOUS AND COMPREHENSIVE EVALUATION

To remedy the main defects in the existing evaluation system we must adhere to continuous and comprehensive evaluation.

a. By continuous evaluation we mean that evaluation should be done continually throughout the learning time. The learning should be objective based.
b. In the present system, the teacher must evaluate the work of the students at regular intervals. But, the evaluation should not only be for the memorization of some facts but preferably goal oriented. The goals may be defined in behavioural terms.
c. The comprehensive evaluation refers to the evaluation in all the domains—cognitive, affective and psycho-motor. It should be about all the abilities as well as values and attitudes of the students.
d. The evaluation in cognitive domain is easier. There is difficulty regarding evaluation of feeling, attitudes, action or activities.

17

Teaching Learning Process

CONCEPT OF COMMUNICATION PROCESS

a. The early meaning of communication is derived from the Latin word 'Communicare'. Communicare means 'to make common'. This meaning has now undergone many changes.

b. Communication is defined in terms of "influence of a system and or mind on the destination and or another mind."

c. Schramm is a noted communication theorist. According to him. "It is the sharing of an orientation towards a set of informational signs."

SIGNIFICANCE OF COMMUNICATION

No effective learning can take place without a proper communication. It may be true that some learning do take place through individual's own efforts in the process of his attaining maturity. As the child matures he learns through his experiences. But, this learning is by and large rudimentary.

SIGNIFICANCE OF COMMUNICATION PROCESS IN TEACHING-LEARNING

a. Teaching-learning process is entirely dependent on communication.

b. The process of communication involves teacher and taught.

c. The input in this process is knowledge, skills, standards values of the society, put in a particular subject matter.

d. The teacher supplies this input and manages it. The significance of the communication process is that the input supplied by the teacher is transmitted to the pupils who benefit by it.

e. The pupil learns through these inputs communicated by the teachers through the process of communication.

TEACHING OF COMMUNICATION PROCESS

The communication at work involves more than receipt. There is also an expectation of understanding, acceptance and action. Hence, in the teaching of communication process it must be realized that it is not simple conveying of message to another person.

In workable communication the sender and the receiver both expect that they will understand each other. Communication takes place when there is acceptance of each other.

FACTORS OR CAUSES AFFECTING COMMUNICATION

There may be described three broad factors which facilitate communication is essential.

a. Physical or environmental factors-like noise, physical distance etc.

b. Personal or Socio-psychological factors like personality.

c. Semantic factors like verbal messages.

An effective communication process is idea centered rather than word centered.

Listening is involved in effective communication process. It is necessary that the teacher is an active listener for which he should be trained. He must develop learning process.

18

Instructional Technology

INTRODUCTION

Speaking educational technology we think the application of technology in the method of education. One of its form is instructional technology. By instructional skills we mean all those techniques of instruction which are used in instruction or teaching. In this chapter we all clarify the term of instructional technology and discuss its basic features.

DEFINITION OF EDUCATIONAL TECHNOLOGY

1. According to G.O.M. Leith : "Educational technology is the application of scientific knowledge about learning and the conditions of learning, to improve the effectiveness and efficiency of teaching and training."
2. In this context J. R. Goss says "Educational technology has to be seen as part of a persistent and complex endeavour of bringing pupils, teachers and technical means together in an effectual way."
3. Sampath opine that "Educational technology implies a behavioural science approach to teaching and learning in that it makes use of pertinent scientific and technological methods and concepts developed in psychology, sociology, communication, linguistics and other related fields."

INSTRUCTIONAL TECHNOLOGY OR TEACHING TECHNOLOGY

We use the terms teaching technology or instructional technology along with Education Technology in relation to teaching-learning process. According to Bhushan and Ahuja there are five different but mutually interconnected terms of educational technology. They are as under :

1. Educational Technology – Educational Psychotechnology: It emphasizes the use of psychology in the teaching-learning process.

2. Educational Technology - Educational Information and Communication Technology: It refers to designing and use of instructional material for communication. This concept of educational technology is more relevant to distance education where the learners are tutored through electronic media or through correspondence.
3. Educational Technology - Educational Management Technology: This concept of technology refers to the use of technology in educational management.
4. Educational Technology - Educational System Technology: The concept of technology is that of applying system theory developed in Engineering to the Educational System which may be as small as instructional technology and may be as big as National System of Education.
5. Educational Technology - Educational Planning Technology : In this term of educational technology the application of technology is in institutional or National Planning. In such a planning specialized services may be required.

HARDWARE AND SOFTWARE APPROACH

The hardware approach is that in which the electronic equipment is used for instructional purposes. The software approach is directed towards the systematic evaluation and refinement of learning structures and properly sequenced instructional material.

From the functional point of view teaching is considered as system. As a system it consists of three variable. (a) Input Variable (b) Process Variable and (c) Product Variable.

The Instructional Methods are concerned with the ways and means of transmitting the content of the subject-matter or the skills to the learner.

19

Socialization and Education

SOCIALIZATION STANDS FOR

Socialization is a social process, and it has been differently defined. Some of these definitions are the following:

1. V.V. Akolkar : The process of adoption by the individual of the conventional patterns of behaviour is described as his socialization, because it occurs on account of his integration with others and his expression of the culture which operates through them."
2. E.A. Ross : The development of the feeling association and the growth in their capacity and will to act together."

THE PROCESS OF SOCIALIZATION

Individuals influence each other by limitation, suggestion and sympathy, besides which the process of socialization is furthered by many social institutions. Man is the product of many social processes such as praise and blame, co-operation and conflict, submission and ascendancy, and these forces create the individual's personality. Education is the most pivotal agency of socialization available to any society.

SOCIALIZATION IN THE FAMILY

The family plays a very significant part in the individual's socialization because the child spends his early formative years in the home. He learns much by observing the people around him, by imitating them, by indulging in activities which win their approval and avoiding those which bring their disapproval and immediate punishment. It is the family environment which can create good habits in him, because the child's moral code is conditioned by the system of reward and punishment which prevails in the family.

The family plays a very important the most significant role in the individual's betterment. Freud and other psychoanalysts believe that the impressions made upon the child's mind at home determine the child's personality as an adult, for in childhood, the child's mind is very flexible and susceptible to any influence.

SOCIALIZATION IN THE SCHOOL

After the home, the child is exposed to the school which also effects him, for the school is nothing less than a miniature society to him. It socializes him, gives him an opportunity to manifest his qualities, instincts, drives and motives, and helps to develop his personality. For the child, the educator's personality and character provide a model which he strives to copy, thereby consciously or unconsciously moulding his personality.

PROCESS OF SOCIAL DEVELOPMENT

Education plays a vital part in the child's social development at every stage, but this education is not the formal education the child derives from books and lectures. It covers the education that comes to the child from extra curricular activities, the atmosphere of the schools, rules of behaviour in the school, radio, cinema, magazines, newspapers etc. Group camps always have a good effect on the individual's social development, for it helps to build his character and also develops many social qualities.

CRITERIA OF SOCIAL DEVELOPMENT

According to Bridges, the following points can help to reveal the extent to which a child's social development has taken place, it at all. Positive answers indicate development, while negative ones indicate the opposite.

a. Played with another child.
b. Spoken to another child.
c. Occasionally made social contact by touching or pushing a child.
d. Imitated other children's actions.
e. Imitated children's laughter.
f. Often spoke to other children.
g. Originated new play activity with other child.
h. Joined group of children in play.
i. Sought another child's approval.

20

Education for Citizenship

WHAT IS A STATE ?

"The state is a politically organized people of a definite territory". **BLUNTS CHLI**

Man is by nature and necessity a social animal. Man cannot live without society. Every man is member of one state or another.

It is very essential for the student of political science to make a detail study of state, because the basic subject of political science is state.

The word "state" is used in different classes of writers. In popular language it is often used discriminately in the place of government.

It is also applied to countries which have no claim to be regarded as state property. This is the case with the state of India. It is necessary, therefore, to correct the definition of state.

STATE-ETYMOLOGY OF THE WORD STATE

Word ''state'' has originated from the Latin word "state", which means the "**social status of an individual**".

In ancient times, no distinction was made between state and society. Hence the word "State" was used to connote social status.

But gradually, its meaning has changed and during Cicero's time, it came to be known as the 'whole society'.

STATE AND EDUCATION

The relationship between the state and education, one must see the extent to which the state can play a part in social atmosphere. In other words, one must see how far education is a subject of state control, guidance and assistance. In modern societies, one finds that education is provided in government controlled institutions as well as privately managed institutions.

Many educational institutions are also controlled and managed by religious institutions. And even among the government of state controlled institutions, one finds that some are administered by the central authority and others by state or local self governing bodies. Another aspect of the state control of education is to determine the spheres which the state should take under its own wings and the arenas which can be safely left to the control of the people.

RIGHTS OF THE STATE

Before discussing the rights of the state with respect to education, it is necessary to know that there is considerable difference of opinion on this subject.

Individualism

Hobbes, Locke, Bentham, J.S. Mill and Herbert Spencer attached greater emphasis to the individual than to the state in the organization of society.

Hobbes favours the policy of Laissez Faire, and suggests that the administration of education should be left to independent citizens.

Collectivism

Collectivist thinkers oppose the views of the individuals. This school of thought has been subscribed to such eminent thinkers as Matthew Arnold, Carlyle, Ruskin, Edmund Burke and others. Caryle and Ruskin vigorously opposed the concept of laissez faire, and suggested in contrast a complete state monopoly of education.

Totalitarianism

Collectivist thinking in its extreme form becomes totalitarianism, which theorizes that the state is the most comprehensive form of human communities.

Pluralism

Propounders of this philosophy want to delimit the powers of the state by a written constitution, for they are in favour of the independence of citizens.

Anarchism

Thinkers belonging to this philosophy are opposed to the existence of any kind of governmental or state authority in society, and for that reason the important question of state control of education does not arise. Anarchism argues, from the absence of any central authority, that the individual's development is best achieved in a condition of complete freedom.

Welfare State

Most of the views expressed above are extremist in nature. The term of the welfare state is an step at achieving some balance between the widely divergent views about the authority of the state expressed in these philosophies.

21

Education for Human Values

WHAT ARE THE VALUES?

Values relate to the aims and objects of human life. For the achievement of the aims men frame certain notions and these notions are called 'values'.

According to Mr. Henderson, "It has been pointed out that man acts to satisfy his wants, anything which satisfies a human want becomes thereby a value. To say, that our conduct is motivated by our values is another way of saying that we act to satisfy our wants."

VARIOUS THEORIES OF VALUES

Educationist have propounded the following theories about the determination of values:

a. Hedonistic view of life : The value of a thing is due to the fact that the thing has power to satisfy our wants.
b. Perfection theory : Anything has value if it relates to the perfection of life for which a man endeavors in his life.
c. Utility theory : Anything which has utility is valuable.
d. Order theory : Anything which is helpful in organizing society is called value.
e. Existence theory : Value is helpful in existence.
f. Experimental theory : Values experiments in present and past as well.
g. Part and whole theory : Values are felt sometimes partly and sometimes wholly.
h. Objective and subjective theory : Values are determined by the notions of individuals and also by the circumstances in which he lives.
i. Emotive theory : Man's emotions are expressed by his nature. These emotions change according to the circumstances. Thus by virtue of his emotion man determines his values.

EDUCATION AND VALUES

According to Reid, "Education is part of life, and clearly our questions about values and education are insuperable from questions of values in life. Values are embodied in educational practice." Thus, education develops a sense of discrimination between good and bad. This discrimination is based on values. These value are tested in schools.

CONTRIBUTION OF EDUCATIONAL VALUES

Educational values contribute the following advantages or opportunities for individual and social life –

a. Betterment of healthy and balanced personality.
b. Capacity to earn livelihood and acquire prosperity.
c. Betterment of vocational efficiency.
d. Creation of good citizenship.
e. Re-organizations and re-construction of experience.
f. Adjustment with the environment and its modifications.
g. Fulfilment of the needs of man.
h. Development of character.
i. National integration and national development.
j. Leaders and skilled workers.
k. Promotion of social efficiency.
l. Cultural values.
m. Utilization of leisure.

MORAL EDUCATION

The aim of education is the complete development of the child, a development in which moral development occupies pivotal place. Man's greatest characteristic is the sum total of an individual's insistent, the inclinations of his mind. Man is made by his thoughts. One finds that children develop characters according to the ideas presented to them during their growth. For this reason they should be initiated into the ideals of sacrifice, hard work and contemplation.

According to Sri Aurobindo, moral education is the education of the heart, without which no individuals can be completely human. But, this moral education cannot be imparted though lectures and text books because the basis of this educations is proper feelings, proper conduct and the development of proper habits of thought, feeling and action.

CONCLUSION

From the foregoing discussion, it is evident that moral education is as much a part of education as religious education is. Hence, moral values relate to the aim of human life.

22

Education for Modernization

MEANING OF MODERNIZATION

The most significant function of education is modernization. Modernization is a comprehensive term aimed at capturing, describing the transition of a society from medieval to modern culture. It stands for development beyond tradition. Modernization, according to some sociologists, is based on European and American models.

As compared to urbanization, Industrialization, Westernization and Europeanization, modernization presents a more complex method and a more complex result. In the intellectual sphere it is an awareness that it is possible to see a rational explanation of physical and social phenomena.

CULTURE OF MODERNIZATION

The highlighting feature of modernization as related to education is cultural. In cultural sphere its symptoms have been pointed out by A.R. Desai as follows –

a. Growing differentiation of the major secular or cultural system, 'The spread of literacy and secular education : A more complex intellectual and institutional system for the cultivation and advancement of specialized roles based on intellectual disciplines'.

b. Emergence of a new cultural outlook characterized by emphasis on progress and improvement, on happiness and spontaneous expression of abilities and feelings, on the development of individuality as a value, and efficiency.

MODERNIZATION THROUGH EDUCATION

Education is the most important skill of modernization since modernization covers the following –

a. Directed change in the system of attitudes, faiths beliefs and values and also in the institutional complex, to expand the acceptability of modern technology and its organizational and operational framework.

b. Growth of the infrastructure essential to the adaptation to technology of foreign origin to specific national needs.

MODERNIZATION OF INSTITUTIONAL EDUCATION

Researches have been conducted in West and India about the contribution of educational institutions in bringing about modernization. Most of them have shown a positive co-relation between the two. However, Saunders in his study Education and Modernization in Brazil has found that it undermines modernity.

SCHOOL AND MODERNITY

Examining the immediate effects of schooling on people's modernity Armer and Youtz conclude, "Western education leads to the modernization of perspective in traditional, non-industrial societies." After a study of 591 seventeen years old males in Kano City in Nigeria they maintain, "western education does, indeed, have a definite effect on value orientations of youth that is largely independent of test factor."

HIGHER EDUCATION AND MODERNIZATION

Besides the relation of schooling and modernization researches have been conducted about the effect of higher education on modernity. Williamson studying University students in United States, Germany, Japan and Columbia concluded that while Americans and Columbians are at the conservative the Japanese are on the other end of the scale of rationalism-traditionalism developed by Kahl.

MODERNIZATION FUNCTION OF EDUCATION

S.N. Eisenstad has rightly out, "Perhaps the best standpoint for the analysis of the characteristics in the education institutions in modern societies is the pattern of demand for and the supply of educational services that tended to develop with modernization".

23

The School and Society

RELATIONSHIP BETWEEN SOCIETY AND SCHOOL

A group of people living together in a particular place is called society. Society is a system or organization of mutual relations between human beings, implicit in certain communities and institutions. The school is a group and education an institution. Really speaking, the school is an important part of society. Here, we mean a specific society, not the general term of society. And a specific society implies a group of human beings living within the limits of a definite country and which is characterized by a specific culture and traditions.

ROLE OF SCHOOL IN SOCIETY

Describing the co-relationship between society and school, T.P. Nunn, the famous educationist viewed, "A nation's schools, we might say, are an organ of its life, whose special function is to consolidate its spiritual strength, to maintain its historic continuity, to secure its past achievement, to guarantee its future".

a. Keeping Moral Power : Schools keep the moral power of the society secure, and also maintain the social heritage of society. This social heritage is handed on by the schools to the following generation.

b. Protection of Historical Continuity : Schools protect the historical continuity of society. Schools perform the function of acquainted the new generation with the ancient myths and legends, and maintaining the pattern of behaviour in the form of traditions and customs.

c. Protection of Social Heritage : Schools also help to keep alive the society's achievements in the past, and transfer it to the younger generation through the teaching of history and the social sciences.

d. Guardians of Future : Schools are the guardians of society's future, because educates are the future leaders of the nation. Schools shape the future of the country by achieving the complete development of these leaders.

e. Literary Function : Through the medium of the schools, the members of society are acquitted with those motives, ideas and inspirations which formed the basis of all the literary achievements of the past.

f. Instrument of Social Change : Schools also encourage considerable discussion and exchanges of opinion on the functioning, methods of working, customs and traditions existing in various parts of the society.

PIVOTAL IMPACT OF SOCIETY ON SCHOOL

It is evident from the intimate relationship that exists between society and school that both influence each other. The various points to be noted in the impact of society on school are the following:

a. Impact of Family : All the individuals, educators and educands, found in schools come from society, and hence, it is only natural that their thinking should influence life in the schools. It is generally accepted that the kind of family an educand comes from can be judged from his conduct in the school.

b. Impact of Social Change : Society is a dynamic and changeable structure. One can see effect of various social changes on a school.

c. Impact of Social Mores : Social conduct in society also has an influence upon the conduct of educand in schools. If social conduct deteriorates, there is no way of shielding the student from this deterioration and consequently conduct in school will also reflect a fall in standard.

d. Impact of Social Needs : The curriculum of the schools is determined according to the needs of society, because parents always send their children to school in order to prepare them for society. They are given education so that they may become useful members of the society.

e. Impact of Social Institutions : The life of the school is profoundly influenced by all the major institutions of society, as family, religion, and economic institutions. From this standpoint one can compare the schools in Communist Russia with the schools of Democratic America.

EFFECT OF SCHOOL ON SOCIETY

Society is influenced by the school in as great a measure as it itself influences schools. In this regard, the following points are to be considered as impact of school on society.

a. Leaders : Schools create the future leaders for all the shares of society. It follows that the type of school will determine the calibre of leaders, and their calibre in turn will determine the nature of society that they will create.

b. Social Control : The school, like the family, is a social institution which socializes the individual and provides him some experience in social control. Hence, the individual will learn to accept the kind similar social control from society.

c. Social Change : It has already been stated that the school plays vital part in social change because it subjects all the customs, traditions, mores, practices etc. of society to continuous criticism.

24

The College in the Social System

WHO WILL GO TO COLLEGE ?

So many brilliant boys and girls have to stop their studies after high school due to lack of facilities. Hence, who will go to college also depends on the facilities offered by the government and the colleges. Besides, the poor parents cannot tackle the expenses of college education.

TYPES OF COLLEGES

The most important types of colleges may be divisioned as follows –

CATEGORIZATION ACCORDING TO ACADEMIC LEVELS

1. Degree Colleges : As is clear by the term, these colleges provide education up to degree level in arts, sciences and technical subjects.
2. Post-graduate Colleges : As is clear by the nomenclature, these colleges provide education in humanities, sciences, commerce, engineering and medicines up to postgraduate level.

CATEGORIZATION ACCORDING TO TYPES OF EDUCATION PROVIDED

1. Arts Colleges : These colleges provide education in arts subjects such literature, economics, political science, geography, history, psychology, sociology, anthropology, education, ethics, value education and languages etc.
2. Science Colleges : While the arts colleges prepare for B.A. and M.A. degrees, the science colleges prepare for B.Sc. and M.Sc. degrees.
3. Commerce College : The colleges provide commerce education to B. Com. and M.Com. students.
4. Medical Colleges : These colleges provide education in different branches of medicine, organized in separate and independent departments under a head, one or two

professors, one or more readers and several lecturers, well equipped laboratories and libraries and the attached out patiently departments with all the facilities for practical medical training.

5. Colleges of Education : These colleges prepare for D.Ed., B.Ed., M.Ed. and other degrees required for trained teacher.
6. Law Colleges : These colleges prepare for LL.B. and LL.M. degrees. Most of them work in the evening because a good number of students are employed during day time.
7. Technical Colleges : Colleges of engineering are the most developed, richest and the most important colleges in a country. Their staff is highly paid and well qualified.
8. Specialized Colleges : Besides the above categories of the subjects of the teaching, there some specialized colleges, teaching special subjects such as management, home science, performing fine arts, music, dance, acting, photography, painting etc.

COLLEGE IN SOCIAL PROCESS

In the social method of a society the college occupies a very pivotal place. It provides trained personnel and developed males and females to the society.

The Technical colleges are connected with the general social structure. Immediately after finishing the colleges studies the boys and girls enter matrimony and professions.

ROLE OF THE COLLEGE

The college expands development of autonomy and the formation of identity. The college provides opportunities of the development of these traits. After leaving the college as a person gets married and establishes his own family he is helped by his training in the college.

SOCIAL STRUCTURE OF THE COLLEGE

a. The Principal : The social structure of the college is organized by the Principal at the apex, the professors, the tutors, the administrative staff and finally the students.
b. Teachers : There is a hierarchy of statues and roles among the teachers according to seniority and administrative matters.
c. University Government : While most of the colleges are governed by rules framed by the university to which they are affiliated, the autonomous colleges are free in their selection of syllabi and mode of examination.
d. Students : The students are the most essential part of the social structure of the college. They are divided into two categories. Those who live in the hostels are called or hostelers, while those staying outside the college are known as day scholars.

25

Freedom and Discipline

DISCIPLINE DEFINED

The concept 'Discipline' is a controversial term. The word 'Discipline' has been derived from the English word 'Discipline' which means 'Willing follower'. Discipline has got a important part in the field of education. It is the foundation upon which the aims of education can stand. A disciplined man means a man having disciplines mind, instincts and habit etc. He is free but does not go beyond limits.

Different scholars, educators and thinkers have explained the term 'discipline' in two ways. In other words, there are two concepts of discipline (a) External and (b) Internal.

EXTERNAL DISCIPLINE

This discipline means some sort of external pose of a boy or girl who is disciplined. Outwardly, he may be disciplined but what about his conscience or heart ? We are not sure about this. This discipline is maintained through rewards and punishments.

INTERNAL DISCIPLINE

The modern educators and thinkers are of the opinion that the external discipline is not the true sense of the term. This type of discipline is not the discipline but a fear or force of the teacher. The students may be disciplined and well mannered, but so far as their attitude or behaviours are concerned, they are unchanged. The real discipline is the discipline of mind, heart, attitude and manner.

DISCIPLINE, ITS EFFECT AND IMPORTANCE

Discipline is the most essential and significant part in educational process. Discipline means whereby children are trained in orderliness, good conduct and the habit of getting the best out themselves. The crucial test of their soundness is whether it represents a real sense, on the part of the children of the rightness of the behaviour that is hoped of them.

KINDS OF DISCIPLINE

The old educationists were of the view that punishment is the only instrument by which a child can be made disciplined. Repression of his impulsive action is only possible through punishments.

According to Adams, there are three main kinds of discipline –

a. Repressionistic
b. Impressionistic
c. Emancipationist

Repressionistic

Repressionistic type of discipline consists of punishment. In order to maintain discipline and make students orderly they were punished for every mistake. This punishment crushed the development of their personality.

Impressionistic

This type of discipline is just the reverse of the above one in respect of its maintenance. If punishment is a part and parcel of the repressionistic discipline, affection and love are the basic points of the impressionistic discipline.

Emancipationist

The supporters of this category are of the view that a child should be left free from both the forces of punishment and affection. He should be given opportunities to progress freely and harmoniously.

COMMENTS AND CONCLUSION

Free discipline can be achieved by allowing complete liberty to the pupils. Free discipline does not mean complete liberty. In the practical field of education, such a proposition is absurd. There must be discipline. The main object of the rules and regulations will be to incite a sense of discipline in the students.

Huxley has aptly remarked : "If your goal is liberty and democracy, then you must teach people the arts of being free, and of governing themselves."

26

Idealism

EDUCATION AND PHILOSOPHY

Philosophy of life speaks us about the aim and objectives of life. Education influence the mind and modifies behaviour to achieve a desired aim or goal. It is a preparation to achieve a certain aim. The aim may be decided by the community is philosophy or country's philosophy or political philosophy of a country.

The following diagram indicates the relationship:

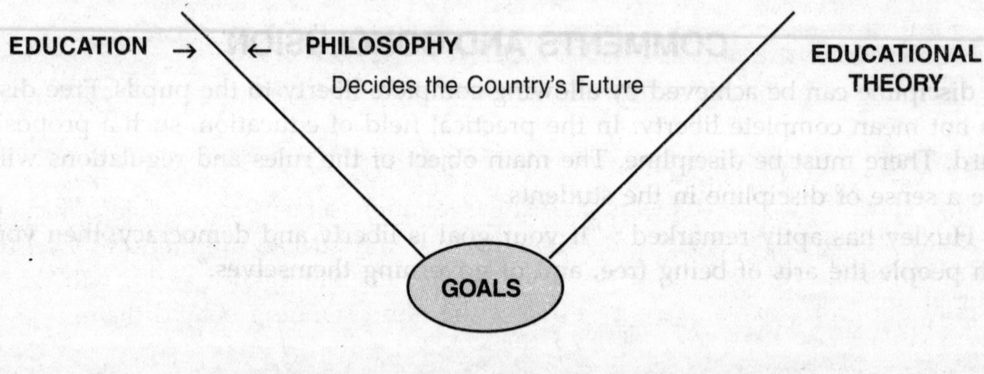

Fig.7. Co-relationship of Philosophy and Education

PHILOSOPHERS ARE THE GREAT EDUCATORS

Great philosophers have been great educators. Great moments in education have been sponsored by those who held a definite philosophy of life. Philosophers who had been really serious about their beliefs, become zealous educationists.

Socrates, Plato, Aristotle, Jesus, John Locke, Jean Tacques Rousseu, G.B.S., H.G. Wells, Bertrands Russle, A.N. White head, Aldous Hurdly, John Dewey and Gandhi in our own days, first preached a way of life and then because educationists.

PHILOSOPHIES AND EDUCATION

Philosophies may differ from people to people, country to country, age to age and will differ the ways to achieve the goal or to prepare men for that goal. So education will be different for different countries. Because their philosophies will be differ.

Professor Ross has rightly said to philosophy and education are the two side of the same coin. Thus, aims of education are directly related to the aims of philosopher of life. Philosophy gives us the theories education those theories in to practice. Philosophy tells us how life has to be lived, education prepares human beings to live that life, to achieve the desired.

WHAT IS IDEALISM?

Broadly speaking, man's life has two pivotal facts - spiritual and material. When the emphasis is on the spiritual fact, it is called idealism to the idealist, 'Mind' and 'Soul' rather than 'Matter' and 'Body' are more important. The idealists idolize the mind beyond everything.

According to Idealism, ideals or higher values are more important in human life than anything else. Idealism is considered to be the oldest philosophy and idea in the world.

IDEALISM DEFINED

In the words of T.S. Ross, "Idealistic philosophy takes many and varied forms, but the postulate underlying all is that mind or spirit is the essential world staff, that the true reality is of a mental character.

Idealistic philosophy believed in the chief values of life; that are truth, beauty goodness and wisdom. According to J.S. Ross, "Goodness, truth and beauty are seen to be absolutes existing in its over right and entirely desirable in itself.

IDEALISM CONVEYS A VARIETY OF MEANING

Idealism concise a variety of meanings, yet the common elements in its philosophical position are that nothing exists except as an idea in the mind of man, the mind of God or in the real of supernatural. It believe the universe has an intelligence and a will that has all material things are explainable in terms of the mind standing behind them.

IDEALISM IN EDUCATION

Idealism in education refers to the idea that educations is a development within and reality is nothing by the self objectives of education are said to be self-realization, an attempt at spiritual becoming. An individual by and large assimilates of its own essential nature. In idealism, complete development permanent importance.

IDEALISM IN THE VALUES OF LIFE

Regarding values of life, Idealism has full faith in eternal and spiritual values of life which never changes at all. Truth beauty and goodness are the outstanding eternal values of life. In Indian idealism, the similar values are there but expressed in other way Satyam (truth) Shivam (*God) and Sundaram (Beauty).

The aim of life is the realization of these spiritual values. It is religion which unifier them all together. These values are not man made by their existence automatic and permanent. Man's duty is to discover these values through a proper education. His discovery is only passing through an awaking of spirit. Invention is beyond the capacity of man.

The idealistic methods of education are many and they were adopted by different photospheres of idealism.

a. Question method, adopted by Socrates.
b. Conversation method adopted by Plato.
c. Inductive and deductive method adopted by Aristotle.
d. Simple to complex method adopted by Desecrates.
e. Concrete to abstract method adopted by Communis.
f. Play way method adopted by Friable.
g. Exercise and Practice method adopted by Pestalozzi.
h. Lecture, debate and discussion method.
i. Story telling and dramatic methods.
j. Correspondence methods etc.

THE CONTENT OF THE IDEALISTIC EDUCATION

The content of the Idealistic education include languages, literature, history, geography, mathematics, science, logic, astronomy, poetry, crafts, health education, etc. which develop (a) Intellectual activity (b) Moral impulses and physical strength. Aesthetic and religious subjects were also formed important part of it. Through these subjects (content) and the methods mentioned above idealistic values could be developed. In India, by questioning, practice, listening, contemplating, analysis and synthesis, the values of idealism could be attained without any difficulty.

MAN POSSESS A 'SPIRITUAL NATURE'

The idealistic believe that man possess a spiritual nature. He has got capacity and power to bring about a new world. He is not helpless like other beings. He expresses his spiritual nature "in the form of intellectual culture, art morality and religion."

CHARACTERISTIC FEATURES OF IDEALISM

The following are the main stand points of the idealistic school of philosophy:

a. Ideas are of ultimate cosmic significance.
b. Emancipation of spirit.
c. Spirit and intellect are of supreme value and not the physical matter.
d. Realization of higher values of life.

e. Ideals are not made but they already exist in the world.
f. Man discovers and not invents those ideals.
g. Man should control the physical environment through his spiritual, cultural and moral possessions.

IDEALISM AND CURRICULUM

As has already been discussed the goal of education, according to Idealism, is to make a man full of ideals. These ideals already exist in the world, why man has to discover them through the aid of education. Curriculum has to be such which should enable him to discover those ideals and then to achieve the ultimate aim.

Curriculum should base an human ideas and ideals. J.S. Ross expresses the view of the idealists in the following words –

"Now a man to be most truly and characteristically human must enter into this heritage of his, reacquiring and recreating the common culture for himself and, if possible, adding something to the common stock.

CURRICULUM BASED ON EDUCATIONAL THOUGHT OF PLATO

Plato was of the view that the curriculum should be formed from the point of view ideas. He said that the highest idea of life is the attainment of the highest good– ultimate truth–God. Hence, the curriculum should be such as to Dewey such qualities in a man by the grace of which he may attain the highest goal that is God.

PRESENTATION OF IDEALISTIC CURRICULUM BY J.S. ROSS

J.S. Ross has divided the human attitude into two parts– (i) Physical Activities (ii) Spiritual Activities.

In the curriculum construction, one must think over these activities and having maintained these activities, subject of study should be given in the curriculum. Physical activities are needed as the subjects of study to faster 'bodily skill" and physical makeup.

On the other hand, spiritual activities imply the intellectual, aesthetic, moral and religious studies.

IDEALISM AND METHODS OF TEACHING

Important characteristics of methods of teaching in idealism are :

a. Learning through reading and self-study.
b. Teaching-learning through talks and lecturing.
c. Learning through memorization.
d. Learning through discussion.
e. Learning through imitation.

DISCIPLINE AND IDEALISM

Important features are –

a. Idealism believes in inner discipline.
b. Idealism advocates cultivation of higher values of life through moral and religious instruction.
c. Idealism accepts restraint on liberty.
d. It requires the teacher to present good examples because the child considers teacher to be an ideal person to be emulated by his pupils.

IDEALISM AND THE TEACHER

The teacher assumes a vital role in the educative process in Idealism. He is the key figure in the educative process. He is the most important element in the educative process. Education according to the idealistic pattern is by and large teacher-centered and not pupil-centered or subject centered. His personality is the most vital influence on the pupils learning manners and above all his character and personality.

DRAWBACKS OF IDEALISM IN EDUCATION

1. Idealistic scheme of education, by and large, pays less attention to physical, industrial, social and electronic environment of today.
2. Emphasis on gaining knowledge is likely to true educational institutions as information longer workshop. School curricular may become overloaded with absolute knowledge sometimes.
3. Idealism may be considered to be automated in the prevailing scientific would-view.
4. Idealistic concepts like 'spirit', 'mind', 'the consumes' have little relevance in classroom teaching.

27

Realism

REALISM MEANING

Realism as a philosophical theory believes that matters has real existence part from our mental perception of it. In this sense, it is an angle of vision according to which things as we see and receive are realities.

REALISM DEFINED

According to J.S. Ross, "The doctrine of realism assets that sphere is a real world of things behind and corresponding to the objects of our perception."

According to Bluffer, "Realism is the reinforcement common acceptance of this world as if appear to us."

Aristotle was a greatest realist in the sense that he condemned the Idealism of Plato. He is regarded as the father of realism.

CHIEF ASSERTION OF REALISM

The following are the main assertions of Realism:

1. Philosophy of common man: Realism is the philosophy of the common man. A common man knows no reality beyond what he experiences. Realism also believes in the reality of the matter.
2. Phenomenally world is true: Realism asserts that there is nothing beyond this world. According to Ross, "Realism accepts only the reality of external world."
3. Sense: The gateways of Knowledge: Realism assets that reality we receive through out senses. Here, Realism comes closes to naturalism.
4. Man: a part and parcel of material world. Realism assets that man is a part and parcel of the material world. He is endowned with sense organs which help his mind to gain knowledge of the real world.

5. Organism: Realists believe that both conscious and unconscious, animate and inanimate things form an organism.
6. Bookish knowledge is of secondary importance: Realists view that bookish knowledge is of secondary importance. Bookish knowledge encourages rote memory.
7. Individuality and sociality: Realistic school of philosophy equally emphasis individuality and sociality. In this sense, the aim of realistic education tends to develop both these characteristics in the child.

REALISM AND AIMS OF EDUCATION

According to the philosophy of Realism education must aim at giving knowledge and understanding of three things –

a. Human nature
b. Human society
c. Human motives

An understanding of human nature will enable the largest to know man's relationship with man and his relationship with nature.

An understanding of human society will enable the largest to know the individual's place.

An understanding of human motives will enable the learners to know how various types of adjustments under different circumstances are possible.

THE AIMS OF REALISTIC EDUCATION

1. Preparation for happy and practical life: Realistic believe that education must not aim at producing just scholars. Rather, it should aim at preparing the child for happy and practical life.
2. Education in cultured values : According to Realism, education must aim at inculcating cultural values among the learners.
3. Understanding the world of living: According to realism, education must with at helping the individual to understand the world in which he lives and to contribute to the understanding of its problem.
4. Developing the childs physical and mental powers: According to realism, human organism comprises both physical and mental powers.
5. Training of senses: Realists believe that a large amount of knowledge of the external world is received through the senses. "Senses are the gateways of knowledge."

REALISM AND CURRICULUM

Realists are highly critical of narrow, bookish knowledge is not conceived by realistic philosophy.

The study of civics should become an important source of giving practical training in citizenship. Above all, Mathematics should be covered to give the young learners an understanding of the world units numerical and spatial sense. An understanding of mathematical concepts should enable the learner to deal intelligently with things in a precise and accurate manner.

REALISM AND METHODS OF TEACHINGS

Observation and experience are the watchwords of realistic education. Realists introduced inductive method of teachings in the process of education.

Realists also advocate the method of learning by doing. But one thing is certain. Whatever is taught and learnt must be done so thoroughly, certainly and dearly.

REALISM AND THE TEACHER

Realistic education assigns fairly important role to the teachers. Teacher who lives by realistic philosophy of humanistic approach, based on intellectual, moral and spiritual culture. Greatest effort of the faecal is that he must adopt his material to the interest of his pupils.

REALISM AND DISCIPLINE

Realists advocate synthetic form of impressionistic type of discipline which should help the child to adjust with the real world. The learner is supposed to follow the code of conduct within school room as well social situations observing the right type of behaviours of his school mates in the other members of society.

PHILOSOPHY OF REALISM

Todays world is a victim of rival political faiths and nations endeavour to secure not the victory of any religions faiths but that of certain. Political faiths, idealism, pragmatism and naturalism are also faiths and determine the course of human life according as men and women abode by them. Realism is also one such belief. It does not in any way arouse any kind of fanaticism but just makes an appeal to human mind for looking at the phenomena of the universe.

CRITICAL REALISM AND NEW-REALISM

In the present scenario realism has acquired two forms. George Sanayana and lovely, for example, belong to the school of critical realists : Montague and perry on the other hand are identified with the school of new-realistic. The difference between these schools are in form only, not in fundamentals. The principal principle of realism in the principle of independence which is not very difficult to understand if we put.

HISTORICAL BACKGROUND

The realistic movement which started from the 16th century was the result of man increased infest in nature. The 16th & 17th century witnessed great inventions and epochal discoveries which greatly increased the store of human knowledge. The rise of scientific enquiry opened new vistas before human mind.

Harveys theory of the circulation of blood. Bacon's formulation and statement of the new scientific method. All phase led to a new spirit of inquiry into the beliefs of nature.

THE CHIEF PEDAGOGICAL IDEA

1. Education 10 per cent from simple to complex and from the concrete to the abstract.
2. Things before rules and words.
3. Students to be taught to analyze rather than to construct.
4. The order and course of nature to be discovered and a method based on this to be applied.
5. Physical education should have a definite aim that of improving health and not only being a gentleman sport.
6. Elements of knowledge should be within the access of all.
7. Latin and Greek to be taught only to those who would complete education but the medium should be the vernacular.
8. Instructions to be given on a uniform, scientific way.

EDUCATION IMPLICATION

Realism taken into account the basic fact of life as they exist believes in that all knowledge in derived frcm experience. Experience is flagstone of what is real. Realism believes in the world of nature. Philosophy away from the world.

So, far as aims of education are concerned, there are two aims of education:

1. Equipping students with knowledge and skills needed to understanding and environment.
2. Enabling student to manage their own affairs. The vocational aims of education is given prominence.

The realistic doesn't attach special importance to the personality of the teacher. Communist was a great realist and his contribution to education is noteworthy.

A CRITICAL EVALUATION REALIZATION

The effect of realism upon university education was not very great. Nor was the influence of the great sense realists immediately felt. In the secondary schools, the realistic tendencies began to appear and science came to be included along with languages in the curriculum. The academies in England and America introduced enriched courses in sciences, masses and the vernacular. Halle was the first to enable the idea underlying realism. But after a short time the movement became general and many German universities created professorship in sciences.

28

Naturalism

NATURALISM – MEANING

Naturalism is mainly concerned with 'natural self' or 'real self'. Naturalists believe that 'material moral is the real world. This real world is governed by the laws. They say that man, the 'creature of the material would, must submit to the laws'. They don't believe in sentimentalism spiritualism and supernaturalism.

The naturalists do not want to see things artificially. 'They want to apprehend reality as it is, in its our nature.' They examine 'self' and say that this 'self' is developed by their Florence of the real.

NATURALISM - DEFINED

Different scholars have defined the term 'naturalize'. According to word, "Naturalism is the doctrine which nature from God, subordinates spirit to matter and sets up unchargeable laws as supreme. In the words of Yoyce, "Naturalism is a system whose salient characteristic is the exclusion of whatever is spiritual or indeed what ever is trescendertal of experience from our philosophy of nature and man".

According to our Indian thinkers, Naturalism is a system that views man and universe as physical, mechanical and biological and not 'Yogical' and 'idiopathically.

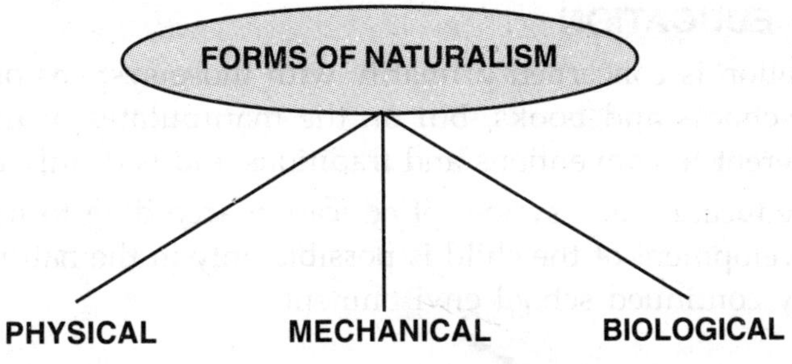

Fig. 8. Forms of Naturalism

PHYSICAL NATURALISM

This naturalism is of physical species. This form explains that experiences are the better products, if supported by naturalism laws.

MECHANICAL NATURALISM

This form of naturalism believes in the fact that man is merely a machine. An eminent naturalist says, "Man is more machine. He is slowly directed by exterior influence. He originates nothing, not ever a thought.

BIOLOGICAL NATURALISM

"Man is the product of evaluation" is the essence of biological naturalism. This form of naturalism which seeks to explain man in terms of lawyer forms of life, is founded on Darwin's theory of evolution. It holds that man has achieved highest form of life in the process of evolution.

ROUSSEASU – THE PROPHET OF NATURALISM

Rousseau (1712-1778 A.D.) is the chief exponent of the philosophy of naturalism. Return to value was the theme of him major work two novels 'The new Helose' published in 1761 and 'Emile' published in 1762. This another book 'Social contract', is a widely read provocative publication.

CHARACTERISTIC FEATURES OF NATURALISM

These are as under –

a. Nature alone is the source of all knowledge.
b. Values are created in terms of specific needs.
c. Natural would is the real world.
d. Mind is subordinate to matter.
e. All real values exist in nature in living close to nature.
f. There is no possibility of any 'supernatural being'.
g. The individuals is always given produce.
h. Man creates societies only to meet some of his needs.

NATURALISM IN EDUCATION

Naturalism in education is concerned primarily with those systems of training which are not dependant on schools and books, but on the manipulates of the actual life of the educand. It is indifferent to conventions and traditions and is deadly against the artificial.

Naturalism in education is a system of education according to nature. The naturalist believes that the development of the child is possible only in the natural environment and not in the artificially continued school environment.

DOCTRINES OF NATURALISM IN EDUCATION

The principles of education that naturalism provides are : (a) follow nature give the child the foremost position in the educative process (c) Let child's nature unfold itself freely (d) Train the senses (e) Make natural impulses, instincts the main instrument of education (f) Make education a pleasure for the child.

NATURALISM AND STUDENT

There are two opinions on this subject -

The first is that of wood worth that the child comes enlightened from heaven but that light is last in this universe. Child is a child but not a developed man.

The second opinion is that of the persons like Sereniah who opines that child is born out of sun and the only educational method is to kill his instincts by keeping him under strict discipline and his direction towards God is the aim of education.

NATURALISM AND CURRICULUM

Naturalist Herbert Spencar has described curriculum according to natural activities of the individual. Man has to protect his life; therefore, he should be given a knowledge of body and health. Home science for family life, social science for social and political life, and literature for art of utilization of leisure.

TRAITS OF EDUCATION

All the recent advances in educational methods have come from naturalism and it is now believed that the only sawed stand point far walking the most efficient method of education lies in the discovery of the nature of the child.

IMPORTANT CHARACTERISTICS OF METHODS OF TEACHING ACCORDING TO NATURALISTS

a. Principle of individual instruction.
b. Principle of learning by doing.
c. Principle of direct experience.
d. Principle of Heuristic method.
e. Principle of examples is better than percept.
f. Principle of acquiring social knowledge by social participation.

NATURALISM AND TEACHER

A teacher is a factor of that defective environment from which a naturalists wants to keep himself away. Hence, he should combine his ideals and laws to himself. But the naturalist forget that the teacher was also a child and as pious as the child.

A teacher hardly gets a place in naturalism. His place is not very honorable rather he is tolerated.

NATURALISM AND DISCIPLINE

Naturalism can give no significance to the idea of discipline in education. Hence, there must be self discipline. Herbert Spencer had advocated discipline through natural consequences.

The naturalist concept of discipline is contained in four words. "Discipline by natural consequences." Basically, when the child runs its head against the table it feels pain the remembrance of pain makes it more careful and so it is eventually disciplined into proper guidance of its. Own movements through natural consequences.

IMPLEMENTORS OF NATURALISM

Rousseau is generally known for this thought. Although Rousseau raised the slogan of naturalism loudly and prominently, he was influenced and inspired by Plato who was an idealist. He raised the structure of naturalism on the foundation of idealistic aims. Brubacher has called him a romantic naturalist.

CHIEF CONTRIBUTIONS OF NATURALISM IN EDUCATION

We have observed that the both Rousseau and Herbert Spencer are regarded as implementors of naturalism. T.P. Nunn is also considered as a strong supporter of naturalism, through sometimes.

Some of the highlighting contributions of naturalism are –

a. Child is a hero in the drama of educational arena.
b. The hero should be allowed to play the dominant role.
c. Hero's need, instincts and aptitudes should be fully met by creating suitable environment.
d. Hero's attitudes and experiences are very pivotal in his education.
e. Hero should be given a lot of liberty.
f. All modern traits of learning emphasis the need of providing advantages for the free play of child's importance.

SHORTCOMINGS OF NATURALISM IN EDUCATION

Some of the highlighting shortcomings of Naturalism in Education are –

a. Absolute freedom to the child is a myth. He cannot be given a long rope to hang himself.
b. Physical nature is not much for obtaining all educational experiences.
c. An extreme form of Naturalism cannot be applied to educational practices.
d. Negative education, but no inducement for doing good deeds.
e. No place of Spiritualism.
f. No definite aim of education. Learning by doing or self-experience good, but no necessary useful.
g. Punishment through natural consequences, not moral and just.

NATURALISM AND INDIAN EDUCATION

Establishment of Nursery, Montessori, Kindergarten, Basic Education schools due to the influence of naturalism. Activity method is a gift of naturalism and how in teacher-training, teachers are given practice in teaching through activities and apertures with minimum of talk. Hence, the very impact of Naturalism is dearly visible in the field of modern system of education.

NATURALISM AND INDIAN EDUCATION

a. Ancient education in free natural environment. Gurukul and Ashrams of the past.
b. Nursery, Montessori and kindergarten schools in different parts of the country due to the impact on naturalism in Indian education.
c. Teacher training institutions based on psychology and child psychology again prove the influence of naturalism on Indian education.

29

Pragmatism

PRAGMATISM MEANING

The word 'Pragmatism' has been derived from a Greek word 'Pragmatikos'. Greek word 'Pragma' means 'work done'. The credit of this 'ism' in philosophy goes to Charles Sanders Pierece (1950). William James, John Dewey and Kilapatrick are the main inceptors of this philosophy.

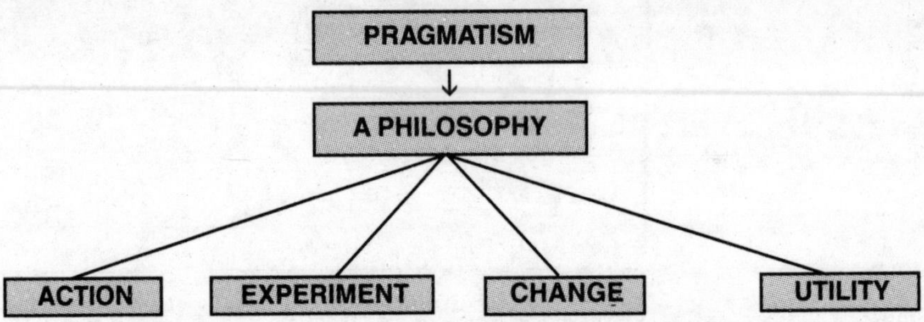

Fig. 9. The Basic Philosophy of Pragmatism

PRAGMATISM – DEFINED

According to Pierce the meaning of this 'ism' to William James is that the aim of man is 'action' William James had analyzed the philosophy of pragmatism and had said that pragmatism is the principle of logical interpretation, the main quality of which is to give practical form to the attempts for the knowledge of truth and if anybody gives a suitable definition for all experimental phenomena which are concerned with regarding or disregarding any concept, then nothing remains in concept.

CHARACTERISTIC FEATURES OF PRAGMATISM

1. This philosophy does not believe in eternal values. Pragmatist Dewey believes only in 'Good' and not in 'Truth' and 'Beauty'. 'Truth' at the time of behaviour is proper. In behaviour, attention should be paid to proprietor. The scientific decision of naturalism are not regarded impartial and natural pragmatism.
2. Conceptualism and pragmatism are against naturalism as the latter does not pay attention to man's purposes and intentions.
3. The Pragmatist does not believe in science and scientific facts as he only believes in the practical form of knowledge. Hence, it is his belief that knowledge is helpful in changing the environment.
4. It goes against conceptualism by talking of good or bad behaviour as a result of truth measured by behaviour and purpose, and joins the compare of naturalists by showing equality in men and animals as far as logic and knowledge are concerned.
5. They go against the idealists by regarding knowledge negligible and 'poyche' free.

FUNDAMENTAL PRINCIPLES OF PRAGMATISM

The basic principles of Pragmatism are:

1. Knowledge of truth is impossible.
2. We can approach knowledge by testing hypothesis through experiment.
3. Truth is proved and made. If truth is useful, it would be our duty to accept it. The quality of a thing can be decided by its consequence.
4. Prior imagination of the ideals and aims of our life is impossible change is its main reason.
5. In a pragmatic society rules, bondages and traditions are changeable because their block the path of progress.
6. Man does creative work; he has also got a role in the creation of truth and values.

PRAGMATISM IN EDUCATION

There are three aspects of Pragmatism:

a. Humanistic Pragmatism
b. Experimental Pragmatism
c. Biological Pragmatism

Humanistic Pragmatism means that every act should be for the benefit of man.

The second and third practical aspects of Pragmatism believe in truth by proved by experiment and change according to environment. John Dewey advocates that the progress of the universe is based on truth proved by experiment.

SHORTCOMING OF PRAGMATISM

1. Pragmatism has proved itself an incomplete philosophy by its indefinite aims by attaching more importance to means rather than ends and advocating the principles like the creativity of man in the field of values.

2. The creation of truth and beauty of the child seems to be a little confusing. It is not always possible to reach by induction without deduction.
3. The significance of education does not lie only in its being helpful in the fulfilment of individual's desires. Man also needs as knowledge by which he may simply feel pleasure.
4. The Pragmatism philosophy of education, by and large, ignore the place of spirit.

PRAGMATISM AND AIMS OF EDUCATION

Philosophy is the background of the successful experiments of education. Often it is said that the pragmatists do not agree with the fact that education takes incentive from philosophy but on the country they believe in the principle that philosophy takes incentive from education. Education and life are one. Philosophy can be wisely applied to education only when its growth is regarded as the foundation of life.

PRAGMATISM AND TEACHER

The work of a teacher has increased with the complication of civilization. Now education without rules cannot be believed in. But a definite education with rules in necessary. School is an easy form of external environment. The teacher has to see that the causes checking the development of the child are removed from his way.

PRAGMATISM IN SCHOOL CURRICULUM

There are many subjects in curriculum which according to core-curriculum should not be different. Curriculum should be in terms of such activities which might be acquired in near future. It means that society is to be mirrored in school. The situation of society is to be created in school. History should be taught with a view to gradual development and as a social science. A knowledge of history enables us to regulate and control economic.

PRAGMATISM AND METHOD OF TEACHING

Education in the activities helpful in search of truth should be imparted to the student.

Education up to recent times has been very strict and definite. A great deal of material, movement, freedom etc. are needed for knowledge. Acquisition of the units of new experience, away from the division of class and times is the best method of education.

The Project method is a gift of pragmatism. Rousseau had also thought over thus project method and had admitted is as a very suitable method of teaching for the age group of 12 to 15 years.

We cannot centre education around the activity alone because often things are memorized through cramming. It is for the above reasons that Pragmatic method of education is one sided and imperfect.

PRAGMATISM AND DISCIPLINE

The child is naturally controlled in social environment, freedom and creative activities. Development of the qualities like self-dependence, sociability co-operation and sympathy is natural. His instincts would be automatically improved.

SCHOOL AND SOCIETY IN PRAGMATISM

The main characteristic of pragmatism is its belief in change. Everything is a flex only the power of solving permanent tendencies and problems would have to be admitted as the true consequence of education. School is the representative of society.

AIMS OF EDUCATION IN PRAGMATISM

a. Social efficiency is the primary aim of education.
b. Holds that aims of education change with the changing times.
c. Stresses more and more education and continuous growth.
d. Regards adaptation to environment as one of the chief aims of education.

HIGHLIGHTING FEATURES OF PRAGMATISM IN EDUCATION

Broadly speaking, the real features of pragmatism in education are:

a. Values are created through environment.
b. Child learns by doing more than by reflection.
c. Curriculum has to be activity-centered.
d. Project method is the main method of teaching.
e. The teacher has to play a very pivotal role in the educational process under pragmatism and he has to be very alert.

PRAGMATISM METHOD OF TEACHING LEARNING

a. Pragmatism advocates devising new method of teaching in the light of real life situations. Such a method should be devised that makes the learning process purposive.
b. Learning by doing, or learning through one's own experience.
c. Project method has been advocated which lay stress on its principles.
d. The method should integrate and co-relate activities.

INDIAN EDUCATION AND PHILOSOPHIES OF EDUCATION

All the four philosophies of education have exercised their influence on the system of education in India. In the past, idealism was the most pivotal philosophical ideology. It is still given prominence in the relation of the teacher and the taught.

At the same time Pragmatism determiners the contents of education. Utilitarian disciples (subjects) are being given more importance.

30

Existentialism

EXISTENTIALISM DEFINED

Existentialism is the youngest philosopher. According to Dr. Radhakrishnan "Existentialism is a new home for an ancient method". It is a modern 20th century philosophy. They know that physical reality exists hence they revolt against system building attitude of Plato.

Meaning of existence comes from two German words "Ex-sister" which mean that which stands out, that which emerges, Existentialism is "Existence precedes essence." The self is a universal essence.

Dr. S. Radhakrishnan : "Existentialism is a new name for an ancient method."

CHIEF CHARACTERISTICS OF EXISTENTIALISM

Criticism of Idealism: Existentialism has emerged and developed as a reaction against idealism. Existentialist philosophers are highly critical of idealism and conceptualism.

Criticism of Naturalism: The existentialist philosophers are critical of the philosophy of naturalism. According to naturalists, life is subject to the universal law of causation. According to the law of causation whatever happens is due to enticement causes and there is no event which can appear suddenly without some of the other cause.

Criticism of the Scientific Philosophy: Besides being critical of idealism and naturalism the existentialist philosophers are also critical of scientific conceptualism. Science abstracts from the immediate data and brings them under some universal law or general rule, whereas, according to existentialists, all abstraction is false, reality in the immediate data only.

Born of Despair: As has been indicated above, on account of an unparalleled development of science and technology, huge industrial complexes and townships have spun. Everywhere man is losing touch of nature. In big towns the problems and inner conflicts of man have multiplied phenomenally.

Value of Human Personality: From the observations made above about existentialism, it is clear that existentialism recognizes the paramountcy of the human personality. Really speaking, for an existentialist 'man' is the centre of the universe and nothing else is equal to it.

Significance of Subjectivity: The Danish philosopher S. Kierkegaard has said the truth is subjective, objectivity and abstraction are hallucinations.

No Construction of Philosophical System: From the ancient times philosophers have cogitated and pondered over problems of God, Souls, Space, Time, Physical world, its origin and evolution etc.

Importance on the Problem of Inner Conflict: The chief problem of the modern highly complex world is not ideological but practical. It is neither relevant nor important today to win followers for a particular ideology or theory but to inspire in men a sense of responsibility and liberty.

EXISTENTIAL PHILOSOPHY ON EDUCATION

1. **Self Realization Aim of Education:** The goal of education, according to existentialism, is the realization of inner truth. Contemporary mechanical and industrial life has alienated modern man.
2. **Child-centered Education:** Existential education is child-centered. It gives full freedom to the child. The teacher should help the child to know himself and recognize his being.
3. **Inversion of Realistic Curriculum:** Existentialist approach to education is almost an inversion of the realist approach. In the field of curriculum while the realists exclusively emphasize science, the existentialists find out that science and objective education severe our relation with ourselves.
4. **Self Realized Teacher:** Existentialists are of the view that the teacher creates an education situation in which the student may establish contact with himself, become conscious of it and achieve self-realization.

VITAL ROLE OF EXISTENTIALISM

It developed as a reaction against the contemporary social, economic and political condition in which man has lost his self. This philosophy has widely effected art and literature. In politics, it has stood against war. Its followers are active pacifists. In the field of education the contribution of existentialism is as follows :

1. **Aimed at Total Development:** The existentialists have aimed at total development of personality through educational process.
2. **Importance on Subjective Knowledge:** The present age of science has made too much of objective knowledge, so much so that the term subjective has come to mean unreal, nonsense, ignorant and irrelevant.
3. **Emphasis on Importance of environment:** The present industrial, economic, political and social environment is valueless. Hence, it helps confusion and corruption, contradictions and tensions.

31

Humanism

WHAT IS HUMANISM ?

In modern age the various doctrines related to human life have been developed. Humanism is one of them. Although the doctrine of humanism is believed to originate from northern Italy during the 14th century, it got momentum in Europe by the Renaissance Movement. However, its origin may clearly be traced from the ancient Indian philosophy.

The ideology of humanism was further popularized by the recent researches made in human psychology in the 20th century. Today we find that the doctrine of humanism not only occupies an important place in spiritual life of mankind but is also vigorously propagated by the social scientists, public workers, scholars and intellectuals in the wordily life of human race.

Humanism is the philosophy according to which man is chief in the scheme of things. Man is the only worthy aim of knowledge. Humanism is the criterion to solve the controversies arising in human life.

Human problems, hence, have become central in all serious thinking. This has created a favourable environment for the rise of humanism.

Like other trends of thought, the roots of humanism can be traced in the Greek philosophy and in the ancient thought of India. In the West, Protegoras of Greece declared that man is the step of all things. After Protegoras, the humanist idea could be seen in the thought of sophist philosophers and the ideas of Plato and Socrates.

HUMANISM : ITS MEANING AND IMPLICATIONS

The English word 'humanism' has been derived from the Latin term 'Homo' which means 'human being'. Thus, literally speaking, humanism is the philosophy in which man occupies a chief place. Etymological meaning, however, is not the sufficient meaning of a term, it covers its historical usage as well.

ESSENTIALS OF HUMANISM

The above matter makes it clear that humanism is obviously against all types of super-naturalism or super-humanism. It cannot think any man to be essentially greater than other human beings. In it, the term human welfare means the welfare of ordinary human beings. It does not aim at superman but only at man. Its central standpoint is faith in the dignity of man. Since man is the creature of this earth, humanism is this worldly and against all types of other worldly theories.

CONTRIBUTION TO EDUCATION

1. **Aims and ideals:** According to humanism education aims at man making. It should be secular, rational and scientific. It should aim at the realization of humanist values in the individual and society. According to it the education aims at complete development of human personality.
2. **Integration of other tendencies:** The humanist trend integrates psychological, sociological and electric tendencies in education. It makes human nature the basis of education. In emphasis the value of individual differences education.
3. **Curriculum :** The humanist curriculum is liberal and extensive. Along with science it has arts and humanities and also moral, religious and spiritual subjects.
4. **Method of teaching:** The humanist method of teaching is based upon human psychology. The teacher educates according to the principles of child psychology, development psychology and educational psychology.

INDIA AND HUMANISM

The doctrine of humanism is supposed to be originated and developed from northern Italy during 14th century and later on made more popular by Renaissance and the revolutionary development in the scientific field.

CONCLUSION

The above educational implications of humanism reveal that it is the best blue print for the planning of future education. It is the solid basis for development of values and culture. It is an integral approach to aims and ideals, means curriculum and organization of education. In fact, humanism may be called the future philosophy of education acceptable and required everywhere.

32

Gandhiji's Philosophy of Education

INTRODUCTION

M.K. Gandhi's philosophy of education is a dynamic term. It gives for the fulfilment of men's needs, biological, sociological and psychological. He believed that education should bring about the betterment of the whole man. Such a thing can happen only when the basic needs of the man are fulfilled.

CONCEPT OF EDUCATION

According to Gandhiji, Education is a means to draw out the best from the child and the man, physically, intellectually and spiritually. Gandhiji paid greater importance towards the personality of the educand. He, in real sense, intended at the balanced development of the child, physically, psychologically and intellectually, to enable him to be able to achieve the ultimate aim, i.e. Truth.

AIMS OF GANDHIAN CONCEPT ON EDUCATION

Gandhiji's concept of education has two fold aims of education before it – (i) immediate aims of education, and (ii) ultimate aims of education.

i. Immediate aims of education

Amongst the immediate aims of Gandhiji's education, we have certain aims which are concerned with our day-to-day life. They may be studied under the following points:

a. **The aim of bread and butter:** Gandhiji has provided for economic self-sufficiency in his term of education.

b. **Cultural aim:** Knowledge has its own value. Some time acquisition of knowledge is important in itself. The pleasure that we drive out of knowledge is an aim itself.

c. **Perfect development:** Gandhiji believed that education should try to train various innate and acquired tendencies to bring about a harmonious and perfect development of human personality.

d. **Moral aim:** It is a famous saying that 'if character is lost everything is lost, but character is not built in itself'. Character training, according to Gandhiji, meant the cultivation of virtues of courage, strength of conviction, righteousness, purity in personal life, self-restraint and service of humanity.

ii. Real Aim

Like the ultimate aim of Gandhiji's philosophy of life, his ultimate aim of education is to know God or realize truth. It is nothing, but the aim of self-realization, which has been in vogue in Indian philosophy since long. 'Self realization is the summum bonum of life and education'.

WAY OF EDUCATION

Since Gandhiji had a different goal and term of education, his methods and procedures could not be those that are in vogue in the present day education. He laid great importance on the learning some craft. He thought that education should be craft centered. This craft should employ the manual labour and productivity.

DISCIPLINE

Gandhiji had a different definition of discipline as compared to many of the Western thinkers. He laid stress on 'self-control'. Gandhiji put forward his idea of voluntary discipline. He did not believe in imposition of discipline. On the other hand, he said that in education, stress should be laid on self-discipline or discipline that springs from within.

A CRITICAL EVALUATION OF GANDHIJI'S PHILOSOPHY OF EDUCATION

Gandhiji's concept of basic education has brought about a lot of change in the educational pattern of our country. The primary schools, more or less, all over India, have been converted into basic schools.

Psychology, socially and biologically sound scheme: Gandhiji's philosophy of education is sound in all these three respects. He envisaged the craft-centered education which would respects. He envisaged the craft-centred education which would bring about the intellectual development through purposeful and productive physical activities in the light of social objectives.

Manual work: Manual work not only encourages the physical activities and brings about the physical betterment but also encourages intellectual development.

Opportunity for self-expression: Self-expression is very necessary for the balanced development of the child's personality. Basic education has made ample provision for the creative self-expression.

Provisions for affection and self-respect: Affection, self-respect, creativeness and activity are the psychological needs of the child. This activities bring about the sense of security as well. M.K. Gandhi had the provision for all these in his scheme of education.

Pedagogically sound education theory: Education should be concrete and realistic. Gandhiji's term of education has provision for all these things. The child, after acquiring education, has to play his role in a nonviolent social order.

CONCLUSION

In fact, Gandhiji was an idealist but he wanted to keep his ideals realistic as well as utilitarian and Pragmatistic.

Gandhiji's contribution to the world of education has not only been important but also testing. He was the first man to have realized the condition and circumstances of the Indian way of life and presented a comprehensive scheme of education. If this scheme is fully implemented, it is sure to generate a new light and a new life into Indian society.

33

Rabindranath Tagore's Philosophy of Education

INTRODUCTION

Rabindranath Tagore thought that the goal of education is self realization. He was a poet and a saint, who had, through his imagination and insight, realized the universal soul in himself and nature.

He thought that realization was the goal of education. Because the universal soul is the root of our own soul, man's aim in life is to reach that universal soul of which all human beings are parts. Self-realization amounts to realization of integration with God.

POLICIES OF SELF EDUCATION

Self-education is based upon self-education, and the process of self-realization is as permanent as that of education. What is most important in this is that the educand must have faith in himself and in the universal self underlying his own individual soul. All those actions which provide a natural sense of satisfaction and contentment will expand the educative process. This contentment is the reaction of the soul, and hence not the same as mere satisfaction and pleasure.

Rabindra's concept of self education, the educated had to follow the three following principles:

a. **Independence:** Rabindranath believed in complete liberty of every kind for the educand the freedom of intellect, decision, heart, knowledge, action and worship.

b. **Perfection:** The second active principle underlying self education is that of perfection. Perfection here implies that the educand must try to develop every aspect of his personality and all the abilities and powers with which he has been endowed by nature.

c. **Universality:** Development of the individual remains imperfect and incomplete until he acquires as abiding faith in the universal soul, a part of which exists inside himself. And for this, it is necessary to identity one's own soul with the universal soul.

GOALS OF EDUCATION

According to Rabindranath, the goal of education is self realization. He is a poet and a saint who through his imagination and insight, realized the universal soul within himself and in Nature.

i. **Integral Progress:** Defining the goal of education, Rabindranath Tagore says, "The fundamental purpose of education is not merely to enrich ourselves through the fullness of knowledge, but also to establish the bond of love and friendship between man and man."

ii. **Physical Progress:** Like Vivekananda, Rabindranath condemned the prevalent system of education which partially exercised the intellect only to the entire neglect of the body.

iii. **Mental Progress:** Besides the physical aim of education, Tagore equally lays emphasis upon the mental aim of education. Like Vivekananda he is critical of the prevalent system of education which laid sole emphasis upon bookish learning.

iv. **Harmony with Environment:** The aim of education according to Rabindranath, is the harmony of the educand with the environment. The educand should know his environment and create harmony with it. As the saying of Rabindranath, 'True education consists in knowing the use of any useful material that has been collected, to know its real nature and to build along with life a real shelter for life.'

v. **Earning Livelihood:** About the aim of education, Tagore's approach is realistic. He, however, does not favour the utilitarian goal of education. This is the objection against the imposition of British system of education upon India.

vi. **Multisided Aim:** The above discussion concerning the source of education according to Rabindranath, makes it clean that he is a multisided attack on this problem.

CONCLUSION

Really, Rabindranath Tagore tries to utilize the findings of modern Western education psychology as well as ancient wisdom of India. Besides in his ideal educational system, the educational process is mainly functional with activity as its basis. It requires both the educand and the educator to be always active. In it learning and practice go together.

Rabindranath is against all types of orthodox discipline and corporal punishment. He thought that discipline through rod is not at all necessary in education institutions. It only leads to depression. Rabindranath observes, "I have a deep-rooted conviction that only through freedom can man attain his fullness of growth."

34

Swami Vivekananda

INTRODUCTION

In the Neo-vedanta humanistic tradition of contemporary Indian society Swami Vivekananda presented a philosophy of education for man-making. Amongst the contemporary Indian philosophers of education, he is one of those who revolted against the imposition of British system of education in India.

Vivekananda was severely critical of the system of education introduced by the British in India. He felt that the current system of education did not confirm to India's culture. He indicated out that such an education only brings about an external change without any profound force.

CRITICISM ON PREVALENT EDUCATIONAL METHOD

Against the contemporary educational method, the chief objection raised by Vivekananda was that it turned men into slaves, capable of slavery and nothing else. About the prevailing university education, he marked that it was not better than an efficient machine for rapidly turning out clerks. It deprived people of their faith.

AIMS OF EDUCATION

Self-development: In contrast to the contemporary system of education Vivekananda advocated education for self development. As his saying, 'By education, I do not mean the present system, but something in the line of positive teaching.

Fulfilment of Swadharma: Vivekananda supported the concept of Swadharma in educational process. Every one has to grow like himself. No one has to copy others. It is hence that he condemned the imposition of foreign education.

Liberty of Growth: Vivekananda is against any type of external role upon the child. He is a staunch champion of liberty in education. Liberty is the requirement for self development and betterment. The child should be given freedom to grow, according to his own nature. Vivekananda said 'You cannot teach a child any more than you can grow a plant. All you can do is on the negative side—you can only help. You can take away the obstacles, but knowledge comes out of its own nature'.

Character Formation: Character is the basis of self development. The goal education as self development, hence, leads to the aim of education for character. Defining character, Vivekananda said, "The character of any man is but the aggregate of his tendencies, the sum total of the bend of his mind'.

Hard Work: Character formation, according to Vivekananda, requires hard work. This is not possible by those who have a wish for all types of enjoyments.

Moral and Spiritual Values: Besides hard work, character formation requires traits such as purity, thirst for knowledge, perseverance, faith, humility, submission and veneration etc. These qualities may be developed by the teacher's example and the pupil's effort.

Formation of Good Character: Character is intimately connected with habits. Habits express character. Good habits make for good character. While the contemporary psychologists admit the value of habits in one's life, Vivekananda has pointed out value of habits not only in this life but in lives to come.

Learning Indicated by Mistakes: The child should be allowed to commit mistakes in the process of character formation. He will learn much by his mistakes. Errors are the stepping stones to our progress in character. Strong will is the sign of great character.

WAYS OF EDUCATION

Love: The best source of education, according to Vivekananda is love. Education should be based on love. Love is best inspiration in character building. The child should be taught through love. This is love for men, for human beings.

Help: The task of the educator is to help the educand in manifesting and expressing his abilities and capacities. Education should aid the individual to recognize his cultural heritage and to use it in his struggle of life.

Guidance: Education is not a bed of roses. Every educand has to face problems peculiarly his own. He solves them by his own labour and with the proper guidance of the teacher.

Attention: Attention, according to old Indian thought, is the key to true knowledge. Vivekananda has placed much emphasis upon focusing of attention. It is only after years of attention that a man becomes a scholar and a great scientist.

Brahmacharya: Again, according to ancient Indian thinkers, Brahmacharya or abstinence is the first means of achieving concentration. It gives mental and spiritual powers of the highest kind. It transforms sex drive into a spiritual force.

Discussion: In addition to concentration the other means of education are discussion and contemplation. It is only through these that the educand may remove his difficulties. Discussion should be carried out in an informal environment.

KINDS OF EDUCATION

Science and Vedanta: With the goal of education as man making, Vivekananda developed a curriculum which could lead to multisided and all round development of the educand. He tried to synthesize Science and Vedanta, Modern and Ancient knowledge so that the curriculum may involve whatever is best in these arena.

He thought that the curriculum may involve whatever is best able to achieve the development of every aspect of the child's personality. With this aim in view he laid attention upon the scientific education on the one side and the teaching of Vedanta on the other. According to him what is really needed in India is a harmony between Western Science and Indian Vedanta.

Training in Art: Besides the provision of Science Vivekananda considered Art as an indispensable part of the educational curriculum. Education in science must be supplemented by training in art.

MEDIUM OF EDUCATION

i. **Mother Tongue:** In teaching languages Vivekananda laid importance upon teaching through the mother tongue.

ii. **Common Language:** There should be a common language which is necessary to keep the country united.

iii. **Sanskrit:** The teaching of Sanskrit forms pivotal part of the curriculum envisaged by Vivekananda. Sanskrit is the source of all Indian languages and a repository of all inherited knowledge.

CONCLUSION

The educational ideals advocated by Vivekananda have been supported by most of the modern Western educationists. Education today is defined as the process of all round development of the child.

35

Sri Aurobindo's Theory of Education

INTRODUCTION

Sri Aurobindo was not only one of the greatest philosopher and yogi of his time but too one of the greatest political leaders and social reformer of his times. He was a great patriot whose first concern was always the good of motherland.

EDUCATION FOR HUMANS

Sri Aurobindo's philosophy not only gives an important place to individual and nation but also to humanity. According to him, 'It must be an education that for the individual will make its one central object the growth of the soul and its powers and possibilities, for the nation will keep in view the preservation, strengthening and enrichment of the nation-soul and its drama and raise both into powers of the life and ascending mind and soul of humanity.'

POLICIES OF SWADHARMA

Sri Aurobindo everywhere considers fulfilment of Swadharma as the law of line. Every individual in a nation has to fulfil his Swadharma. The aim of education in a nation is to prepare the individual to serve their roles according to their status in society. Individual differences are the basis of modern system of education. Nature has bestowed different human beings with different capacities and powers. Hence, the educationist has to progress in the child whatever has been already endowed to him by God.

EDUCATION DEFINED

In the words of N.C. Dowsett, the concept of education in Sri Aurobindo's philosophy is summarized thus, "The meaning of the word education is... to educe the inner, hidden, latent, dormant, potential secret within every human being, secret because it is not of the sense but of the inner truth of being and because it is that most unknown part of the being which has yet to evolve to its full stature."

THE REAL EDUCATION

Defining real education Sri Aurobindo wrote, "There are three things which have to be taken into account in true and living education, the man, the individual in his commonness and in his uniqueness, the nation of people and universal humanity."

SWABHAVA AND SWADESHI

Besides Swadharma, the contribution of a nation is determined by Swabhava. Swadeshi was the avowed policy in Sri Aurobindo's political philosophy. Each nation, according to him, has to grow and develop in tune with its peculiar Swabhava and Swadharma. This policy has been adopted by Indian thinkers since olden time.

RATIONAL EDUCATION

It is not like that Sri Aurobindo finds no place for reason in education. In his philosophy everywhere Sri Aurobondo has supported reason like any staunch rationalist and lauded its role as the law giver to the irrational elements, passions, the sensibilities and the sense organs. A real and living education is also a rational education though it goes beyond reason for the spiritual growth of man.

POLICIES OF NEW EDUCATION

Variegated types of educations should not be given successively but simultaneously. The highlight should be all the time on the inner growth. As the educand advances he should be taught to identify his real and to find out the law of his being.

Perfection: Sri Aurobindo was basically a perfectionist. He was never satisfied with partial remedies. It is hence that he left the political arena to pursue a more perfect method of realization of perfection of human race. It is hence that the presents his integral yoga as a solution of the individual needs but also of the social and political chaos facing nations and humanity.

Harmony: Harmony is the basic to understand Sri Aurobindo's thought everywhere. Those who complain about the difficulty in understanding his writing lack this inherent urge to harmony.

Evolution: The edifice of Sri Aurobindo's philosophy is based on his concept of evolution. It stands and fallen with the truth of evolution. Evolution has been felt and realized by almost all the thinkers of our age.

Humanization: Education according to Sri Aurobindo, as according to Vivekananda, goals at man making. The individual and the nation have to grow as members of one humanity. Sri Aurobindo's method of national education ultimately aims at evolution of humanity.

Harmony of the individual and collectivity: While most of the thinkers and educationist in social-political field have either laid attention upon the individual or the collectivity, Sri Aurobindo aims at realization of harmony between individuals and between nations.

Building the innate powers: The chief goal of education according to Sri Aurobindo is, "The building of the powers of the human mind and spirit - the evoking of knowledge and will and of the power to use knowledge, character, culture that at least if not more."

Cultivation of values: The present crisis of man is due to the chaos of values. Old values have been challenged while new values have not firmly taken their place. In his social philosophy Sri Aurobindo has particularly discussed his problem.

CONCLUSION

While Sri Aurobindo outlined a national system of education, a model to realize his scheme was developed by The Mother in the form of Sri Aurobindo international university at Pondecherry. It was developed as a new centre of education to experiment for the realization of the aims outlined by Sri Aurobindo.

36

Educational Psychology

MEANING AND DEFINITIONS OF PSYCHOLOGY

Psychology is the interpretation and expiation of behaviour in mental or psychical terms. It tries to know how we perceive, learn, remember, imagine and think. It is concerned with the child, adult and even with the animal, with the normal as well as the abnormal human beings.

SCIENCE OF SOUL

In fact, the word ***'Psychology'*** has been derived from the two Greek words – Psyche and Logos. ***"Psyche"*** - means ***"Soul"*** and ***"Logos" - means about***. Thus, Psychology means the science of soul.

The word soul has been interpreted differently by different thinkers like – Plato, Aristotle and others. Its use in the field of Psychology will not enable us to explain the modern scientific developments of this subject. As a result, this definition has now been abandoned.

SCIENCE OF MIND

Psychology was defined as the science of mind or as a study of the mental life of the individual. This definition was given up as unsatisfactory because of the following reasons:

a. The mind as an object does not exist, what exists is only the brain.

b. We can study mind only when it functions or operates in human behaviour or activities.

SCIENCE OF CONSCIOUSNESS

Some thinkers like William James define Psychology as the science of consciousness. Consciousness stands for the mental activity which is characterized by the individual, being aware of what is happening. It means that Psychology includes the understanding of the behaviour around us. Therefore, this definition is one sided.

SCIENCE OF BEHAVIOUR

A modern school of thinkers like Watson, defined Psychology as the science of behaviour. The behaviour stands for all visible activities of man which can be put to an experimental analysis.

THE MODERN VIEW

To sum up, we may say in the words of Woodworth "***First Psychology lost its soul. Then it lost its mind. Then it lost its consciousness. It still has behaviour of a sort***". Perhaps, the best description of Psychology is to define it as the scientific study of the individual when his mind and body are working together as a single unit.

MODERN DEFINITIONS OF PSYCHOLOGY

a. *'Psychology is the study of human nature'.* **– Boring Langfeld**

b. *'Psychology is the study of human behaviour and human relationship'.* **– Crow and Crow**

c. *'Psychology is, the scientific study of the activities of the individual in relation to his environment'.* **– Woodworth**

PSYCHOLOGY IS A SCIENCE FOR THE FOLLOWING REASONS

a. Like all sciences it has its theory as well as practical aspects.

b. Like all sciences it uses the scientific method of enquiry.

c. Like all sciences it also emphasizes the search of truth. It studies behaviour and describes the laws governing them.

PSYCHOLOGY- A SCIENCE OF BEHAVIOUR

In modern times the concept of the term behviour has a very wide meaning. Behaviour in its broad sense includes all types of activities - motor activities like walking, speaking, cognitive activities such as perceiving, remembering, thinking or reasoning and effective activities like feeling happy, sad, angry or afraid.

IMPORTANCE OF PSYCHOLOGY IN EDUCATION

Psychology may be defined as study of man's behaviour, experience and his conscious and subconscious life. The term has gone through various definitions and redefinitions. It has been successively defined as the science of mind as the science of mental activity, as the science of consciousness and the science of conscious experience.

CONCERN OF PSYCHOLOGY

Psychology is concerned with whole man: how he feels, behaves, thinks, and experiences. Experience is what man feels. When he cries out of pain, he shows his behaviour by crying and the attached pain is experience behaviour. It is just what we observed.

BRANCHES OF PSYCHOLOGY

We have a number of branches of psychology, such as, child psychology, adolescence psychology, physiological psychology, developmental psychology, general psychology, and clinical psychology and so on. Educational Psychology is also one such branch of Psychology.

CO-RELATIONSHIP BETWEEN EDUCATION AND PSYCHOLOGY

Education is a growth and developmental process. It is a dynamic process of thinking, doing and living. It is a process of achieving maximum social, emotional, physical, intellectual growth and development. It is also a product – a product composed of knowledge, skills, attitudes, habits and ideals.

Psychology as applied to Education helps us understand how the educative process involved in thinking doing and living can be facilitated

MEANING OF EDUCATIONAL PSYCHOLOGY

Psychology of Education or Educational Psychology is an applied science and one of the branches of psychology like social, industrial or clinical psychology. Its main importance is on teaching and learning. Its chief areas of study are : (a) the learner (his nature and characteristics); (b) the learning process; (c) the way in which the learning processes are facilitated by the teacher; (d) the investigation of scientific principles most effective for formal education.

IT DEALS WITH

a. The nature and conditions of the learning method;
b. The educational significance of individual differences in the rate and limit of learning;
c. The most effective methods and traits of learning;
d. The educational implications of transfer of learning;
e. The nature and nurture of intelligence;
f. The group process in the class room;
g. The teacher's personality as a factor in learning.

WITH THE PROBLEM

In solving these problems concerning, education, educational psychology not only draws upon the facts and principles obtained in studies made in psychological laboratories, but also makes her own scientific studies in classroom situations and formulates scientific principles that can guide the teacher to conduct teaching work most effectively.

The province of educational psychology is the whole child. To quote Peele, education has a specific purpose as "***the development of a well-integrated person capable of exercising such responsibility in society as his powers allow.***" Educational psychology contributes to such development which has aspects mental, physical, emotional and spiritual.

EDUCATIONAL PSYCHOLOGY IS AN APPLIED SCIENCE

a. Really, Educational Psychology is an applied science. It applies to the solution of educational problems, facts and principles which act scientifically determined in the fields of pure Psychology and other sciences.

b. The Educational Psychologist has to find out the problems met in education and to see what Pure Psychology has to offer in contribution. Putting these in a reverse order, he has to first see what the psychological facts and principles are and what they imply for educational purpose.

c. Educational practices change with changes in psychological terms and ideas. At one time intelligence was regarded as equally distributed among all children, except among the very superiors developed; a very different concept of the distribution of intelligence came into existence.

d. Educational Psychology is an applied science. But it does not mean that it is Psychology alone whose principles and facts are applied here. Just as Engineering science tries to apply principles of Physics, Mathematics, Chemistry and Geology, so also Educational Psychology tries to solve the problems of education by making use of knowledge from all fields as are related to the problem at hand.

e. Educational Psychology has not only applied emphasis but it also has theoretical emphasis — theoretical in the sense that it forms theories regarding various studies of educational concern.

f. It investigates scientific principles and facts and in the light of those tries to discover and explain the extent to which hereditary potential is effective.

INFLUENCE OF EDUCATIONAL PSYCHOLOGY IN THE TEACHING LEARNING PROCESS

A number of educators and school administrators believe that educational psychology has an ordered catalogue of educational prescriptions and these prescriptions if followed wisely will make them good teachers and efficient school administrators.

IMPLICATIONS OF THEORIES OF LEARNING TO TEACHING

Educational psychology presents various viewpoints of learning and gives their educational implications.

IMPLICATIONS OF TRANSFER OF LEARNING THEORIES OF TEACHING

Education has one of its aims as preparing persons to meet problems of life successfully and the theory of transfer of training gives the teacher a clue how he should teach so that maximum carry-over from classroom situation to life situations may be made of habits, ideals, attitudes and knowledge.

IMPLICATIONS OF PSYCHOLOGY OF THINKING AND PROBLEM SOLVING

If the teacher wants to produce worthy citizens — citizens capable of solving problems, citizens capable of working out a social change, he will have to provide challenging varied problems in the classroom so that ability to solve problems may be developed.

HABIT FORMATIONS

Habit is Second nature and we are all creatures of habit. Habits are flywheels of society. It is very much essential in our day-to-day life.

IMPLICATIONS OF PRINCIPLES OF GROWTH AND DEVELOPMENT

The teacher's responsibility is to stimulate and direct his pupil's growth in physique, mentally, emotional control and social personality.

IMPLICATIONS OF INDIVIDUAL DIFFERENCES

In any classroom there are pupils who are exactly alike. In a class of 40 pupils there are 40 problems, all unique and different.

IMPLICATIONS OF HEREDITARY POTENTIAL

The basic problem of education is to direct hereditary potential-intelligence-for solving problems. The scientific and technological advance made by some western countries is the result of schools maximum direction of human potential.

METHODS GIVEN BY EDUCATIONAL PSYCHOLOGISTS

The educational psychologist - collects reliable data to solve educational problems in number of ways. Valuable data are derived from teaching experience and tentative conclusions are drawn from them. The Educational Psychologist makes use of the following methods to collect reliable data and arrive at scientifically sound conclusions:

1. **Controlled Observation**
2. **Experimental Method**

CONTROLLED OBSERVATION

A number of techniques and skills are used for controlled observation. These involve use of Questionnaire, Clinical investigation, Genetic study and Case study.

MERITS OF CONTROLLED OBSERVATION

Through these techniques the observer makes detailed notes about the behaviour of the child. The details of observation are controlled and placed in a systematic order. The merits of this method are that the whole child is seen in a whole situation.

QUESTIONNAIRE METHOD

A questionnaire is a list of questions framed to discover the behaviour pattern of the child. Answers to these questions are analyzed to draw pertinent conclusion.

CLINICAL INVESTIGATION

When a child is found facing serious learning difficulties or indulged in delinquent behaviour, the educational psychologist makes a careful diagnosis.

GENETIC STUDY

A genetic study is a record of growth over a long period of time. Human physical growth and development, for example, are studied either cross-sectionally or longitudinally.

CASE STUDY

Case study is a comprehensive study of the individual child made to understand him as a whole. It covers all the items of his history from birth onwards.

EXPERIMENTATION

Experimentation involves –

1. Control of variables.
2. Study of one single variable.

In the experimental study the psychologist takes the following steps :

a. He forms matched groups.
b. He treats the two groups differently.
c. He observes the difference in results.
d. He interprets the difference.

EDUCATIONAL PROBLEMS

Some of the educational problems that have been studied through experimentation are the following:

1. Comparative effectiveness of different teaching approaches.
2. Comparative advantages of homogeneous vs. Heterogeneous grouping.
3. Transfer of learning.
4. Optimum class size.
5. Part vs. Whole method of remembering.
6. Relative values of different types of curriculum lions.

LEARNING

Learning according to **Crow and Crow** is acquisition of habits, knowledge and attitudes. The process of acquiring new knowledge and new responses is the process of learning, says Woodworth. Such formal definitions of learning are at best, incomplete attempts to explain briefly an exceedingly complex affair.

Learning is not only getting knowledge of subject-matter or trait in art by study, by experience or by being taught, it is also an acquisition of habits, attitudes, perceptions, preferences, interests, social adjustments, values and ideals.

Even such simple things as learning to spell and add involve a number of forms of learning. We do not know what happens physiologically when we learn to spell or add. Possibly, there is some change in nerve or cell structure when learning of any kind occurs.

Change in behaviour as a outcome of learning occurs in two directions – either it is for improvement or for otherwise. But, improvement of behaviour is usually implied.

Change in behaviour occurs in meeting changed conditions so that obstacles are overcome and homeostasis is maintained. Homeostasis is tendency of an organism to remain stable or seek to achieve balance or stability through its own regulatory action, as regards temperature, body chemistry or psychological conditions.

Finally, we have to say that learning is a change. It is a change in performance through conditions of activity, practice, and experience.

In classroom situations, the activity or experience which leads to change in performance may be telling or listening or judging or reading or reciting or observing a demonstration or viewing a T. V. Lesson or experimenting in the laboratory.

CHARACTERISTIC FEATURES OF LEARNING

For any definition or learning leaves many things unsaid; yet some description of learning process may be given. Viewed in this sense, learning is an event in which the learner tries to adapt his behaviour so as to succeed in a situation which he perceives as requiring action.

Learning is a result of activity: learning process is primarily active. The motivation and goal seeking are at the heart of the learning. The learner changes his behaviour in order to meet a problem raised by his environment. The change comes through experience.

LEARNING IS AN ACTIVE PROCESS

Learning is a result of activity on the part of the organism. We learn by doing.

LEARNING INVOLVES INDIVIDUAL LEARNER

Learning takes place in the learner. The nature of the learner is revealed through a study of individual differences in intelligence, bodily vigour and mental health.

INTERNAL AND EXTERNAL FACTORS ARE INVOLVED IN LEARNING PROCESS

There are internal as well as external factor that effect learning process. There may be a desire in the learner to achieve a certain goal or there may be external motivation on learn.

LEARNING PROCESS IS FACILITATED BY THE TEACHER

Though most effective learning requires learner's individual activity and responsibility, yet a teacher helps the learner in perception of meanings.

SCIENTIFIC PRINCIPLES OF EFFECTIVE LEARNING

The principles of effective learning are as follows. For a better understanding of the principles the reader is advised to go through sections indicated in brackets after each principle listed below :

1. Effective learning results from teacher guidance in the form of useful cues and modes of attack on a problem though the learner may utilize self-discovery of invention or may generalize from past experience.

2. The learner must have suitable abilities and an appropriate background of experience, self-sufficient mental-maturity, readiness to learn. To acquire more effective patterns of behaviour the learner has to make goal-directed provisional trials which should be oriented toward differentiation and integration of better patterns of behaviour.
3. One learns more rapidly when the new has meaning related to the old.
4. The desire to learn facilitates the learning process.

FORMS OF LEARNING

There are a number of forms in which behaviour changes are expressed by organism. The following forms are listed not to show that they are mutually exclusive but to indicate the complexity of the phenomenon of learning.

SENSORY MOTOR LEARNING

Sensory-motor skills are those skills which become so automatic that other learned activities may be pursued with no interference; for example, walking, riding a bicycle, getting dressed, knitting.

PERCEPTUAL MOTOR LEARNING

Perceptual motor skills depend upon perception and association.

CONCEPTUAL LEARNING

Concepts are mental images of a thing or class of things formatted by generalization from particulars. Concepts are characterizations of ideas that are broader and more inclusive than a definition.

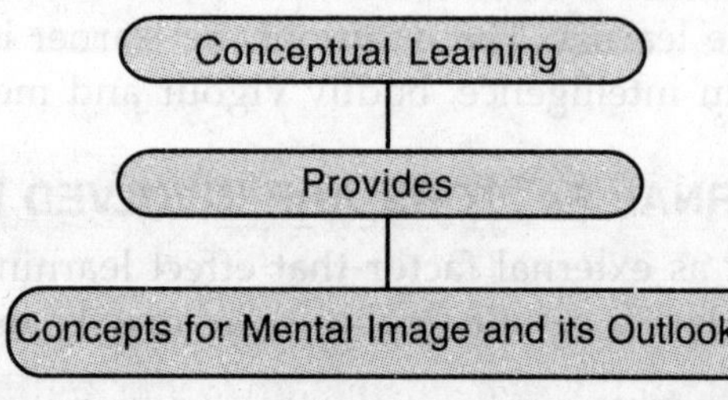

Fig. 10. Concept of Conceptual Learning

ASSOCIATIVE LEARNING

Associational learning is seen in learning vocabulary. A certain sequence of letters is so associated with an object, or a concept of a situation that the sequence of letters tends to recall the object or concept or situation.

PROBLEM SOLVING

A problem has different meanings. It is something difficult and doubtful, something unintelligible.

37

Stages of Development

GROWTH

Growth is conceived narrowly as sheer increase in size but in educational and psychological literature the term includes maturation, development and learning. **Maturation** is the process of coming to maturity or reaching stages of development.

The infant matures in the process of becoming and adult; and the parts of the organism also mature.

How do you differentiate growth and development?

1. Narrowly conceived, growth is sheer increase in size, height, degree, power, etc. For example, growth from conception onwards is a natural thing. It is in this sense used for physical change.
2. As such we speak of muscle growth, brain growth, bone growth and the growth of body in general. The changes produced by growth process accumulate and are measured directly.
3. Development is the direction in which growth takes place as a result of factors outside the maturing individual. In this sense while growth is a natural process; development is a result of the environmental factors that affect the organism as he grows.
4. In Educational and Psychological literature growth includes development as it includes maturation and learning. Growth and development are related because both occur together. Hence, there is a tendency on the part of educationists and psychologists to use both interchanging.

DOCTRINES OF GROWTH AND DEVELOPMENT

The teacher should clearly understand the nature of growth and its principles before he launches upon the task of educating children. These highlighting doctrines are:

1. Growth and development result from an interaction of Heredity and Environment.

2. Growth proceeds more rapidly in earlier years.
3. Growth is continuous and comprehensive and it is gradual.
4. Growth is a regular step-by-step process.
5. Each child and adolescent has his own rate of growth.
6. Growth moves from Generalization to Differentiation and Integration.
7. Traits are correlated as a general rule.
8. Maturation influences the results of training.

These doctrines will be analyzed in detail below because they have a far reaching impact upon principles and practices of education.

GROWTH AS A FUNCTION OF HEREDITY AND ENVIRONMENT

The development of an organism is a product of two interdependent factors- ***'what he is'* and *'what he has'***. 'What an organism is' determined by his hereditary potential and 'what he has' is fixed by his environment.

GROWTH IS RAPID IN EARLIER YEARS

In early childhood any structures and functions grow at a much faster rate and as the child grows, the rate of growth slows down.

GROWTH IS CONTINUOUS AND GRADUAL

Growth or development does not occur in spurts. We may talk of stages of development or of growth as infancy, childhood, adolescence but it does not mean that when one stage stops and other starts. There are no breaks in the process of development.

GROWTH IS A REGULAR STEP-BY-STEP PROCESS

Growth is never haphazard. There is order and sequence. For example, the baby creeps before the crawls, and he crawls before he walks, and the child walks before he runs and he runs before he dance.

EACH CHILD HAS HIS UNIQUE RATE OF GROWTH

Some children grow rapidly. Some are slow. Some travel by an extract, some by a car and some by a jet plane.

GENERALIZATION

Differentiation and Integration in Growth Process: As a child develops in a particular trait, he shows generalized behaviour.

STAGES OF DEVELOPMENT

There are certain distinct well-defined stages of development from birth to death. These are

a. Infancy – from birth to two years.

b. Early childhood - from two to six years.
c. Later childhood - from six to twelve years.
d. Adolescence - from twelve to sixteen or seventeen years.
e. Adulthood - after 18 years.

INFANCY AND THEIR DEVELOPMENTAL FEATURES

a. The stage infancy technically refers only to the first two years of life, but the psychological studies bring it up to the age when the child is developed enough to attend school.
b. The infancy is marked by a continuous growth and development. The neonate is helpless and dependent but gradually he gets control over his physical and motor skills.
c. The most important feature of infancy is marked by egoism. The infants are egoistic in nature.
d. The infants are neither social or unsocial. Similarly, he is neither moral nor immoral.

PHYSICAL DEVELOPMENT

The child develops very rapidly during the infancy stage. At the time of birth, the child remains bodily unattractive because their skin is lined, the face puffed up and red, the size of the head approximately one-fourth of the body and the rest of the body unbalanced.

EMOTIONAL DEVELOPMENT

The emotions of the infants are not specific at birth. The infant can't show any specific emotions like anger, far, joy etc. like the adults. They show random reaction to a stimulus. Gradually they show anger when their freedom is restricted by the adults.

SOCIAL DEVELOPMENT

Social development of infants primarily depends upon his elders and parents. At home, if the parents are well inclined towards him, the infants start developing a healthy social personality.

Education is not only a process of growth. It aims at the fullest possible realization of all the potentialities of children.

FEATURES OF DEVELOPMENT DURING THE PERIOD OF EARLY CHILDHOOD

The following features of development are pivotal during the period of early childhood:

PHYSICAL DEVELOPMENT

The early childhood period is marked by physical growth and motor development. At the age of five years, the child gains about nine inches in height from that of age two. A weight gain of about four or five pounds per year is also noticed. In case of healthy children, the growth is more rapid than the unhealthy children.

MENTAL DEVELOPMENT

Each emotion is distinguished by the type of overt response demanded. Such as - fear arouses crying, grief arouses weeping.

SOCIAL DEVELOPMENT

Home is the primary social environment of the child. It is home where he gets the first lesson of social behaviour and manners. Mother is the first company of the child. Next comes father and other members of the family.

EMOTIONAL DEVELOPMENT

The emotional development takes place during the childhood stage. He expresses his emotions like anger, love, fear etc. in different situation.

MOTOR DEVELOPMENT

There is a lot of motor development during the early childhood period. The child is capable to perform different types of activities like – jumping, running, throwing, walking, climbing, catching, tri-cycling etc.

EDUCATIONAL VALUE

1. Early childhood is an age of rapid growth and development. So, the child should be provided with balanced diet at this stage.
2. The teachers should see that children have proper physical growth and motor development.
3. They should be provided for their continued growth in the school through useful activities and adapting its various programmes according to individual differences.

ADOLESCENCE

Adolescence has been defined as the period or stage of development that intervenes childhood and adulthood. Children have to pass through a stage of development to reach adulthood. In this stage of development they are neither children nor adults, but something else.

The two Themes –

a. When does adolescence begin?

b. When does adolescence end?

ADOLESCENCE AND ARTIFACT OF CULTURE

What we call adolescence is an artifact of our culture. In some cultures the provisional age when a person passes the point from adolescence to adulthood is 15 and in others it is 21.

Defining adolescence as a stage of development different from childhood on one side and adulthood on the other is a little fallacious. Growth or development never takes place in a discontinuous manner. Growth curves, actually have no discontinuity or break anywhere for any but whatsoever.

PHYSICAL DEVELOPMENT IN ADOLESCENCE

If we study the growth curves of height and weight from infancy to adulthood, we find that growth in these physical aspects is rapid in infancy, goes down in middle childhood, and shoots up in adolescence.

THERE ARE CHANGES IN PROGRAMME OF THE BODY AND IN ORGANS AND TISSUES

For Example, the legs grow relatively longer upto 15 years and then stem length increases slowly. In the childhood the whole body becomes slender but in the adolescence it begins to broaden again. The bones increase not only in size but also in number.

One of the Chief Characteristics of Physical Growth and Development of Adolescents is their Variability: For example, you will find in a certain class 50% of the girls having entered the puberty-cycle whereas the remaining 50% has not done so.

EFFECTS OF EARLY AND LATE MATURING ON BEHAVIOUR OF ADOLESCENT

The early maturing boy, as we have said earlier, gets a good position among his associates. Since he is tall for his age, he becomes the leader of the group, and the teacher also assigns him a position of responsibilities.

FEATURES OF ADOLESCENCE

1. '*Adolescence is a period of great stress and strain, storm and strike*'. **Stanley Hall**
2. '*There is one word which best characteristics - change. The change is physiological and psychological*'. **Bigge and Hunt**
3. "*Report there is a tide which begins to rise in the veins of youth at the age of eleven or twelve*". **Hadow Committee**

38

Instincts and Emotions

MEANING OF INSTINCT

The word **"Instinct"** is derived from the Latin word **"Instincts"**, means to instigate 'to motivate'. Later on, it was used in the sense of any natural endowment which enabled a living organism to respond in a certain way without any experience and learning.

VARIEGATED DEFINITIONS

1. Mc. Dougal defines instinct as "an inherited or innate psychophysical disposition which determines its possessor to perceive and to pay attention to objects of a certain class to experience in its presence a certain emotional excitement and to act in regard to it in a particular manner, or at least, to experience an impulse to such action".
2. Woodworth defines instincts as '*Unlearned Motives*'.
3. In the words of Ross, "*An instinct is an inherited or innate disposition which determines its possessor to behave in a certain specific way in relation to specific objects*".
4. Nunn defines instinct as merely phases of will to live.

Among all the definitions, let us analyze the definition given by Mc. Dougal.

a. In the first place, an instinct is an innate disposition.
b. Secondly, in the presence of this instinct the person perceives certain specific objects.
c. Thirdly, an instinct arouses a feeling, an excitement.
d. Fourthly, the instinct stimulates the person to act in a particular way.

NATURE OF INSTINCT

The nature of instinct may be explained in the following way:

1. **Instincts are universal in nature:** Instinctive actions are characterized by certain uniformity. In lower animals, the instinctive behaviour display a rigid uniformity.

2. **Instinctive acts are innate:** They are unlearned or they are not acquired through practice. They are neither voluntary, nor habitual actions, nor automatic imitation of others' behaviour.
3. Instinct is inhabited from the ancestors.
4. **Instinct is a natural innate tendency:** It is an inherited or innate engram-complex or disposition, which determines its possessor to have in certain specific ways. It is not acquired or learned behaviour.

IMPACT OF INSTINCTS

a. Instinct is fundamentally Pivotal in the study of behaviour, and hence they are profound consequence in educational theory and practice.
b. Instinct like gregariousness, curiosity, anger, constructive and sex has immense educational value. They and other instincts supply motive power for our activities.
c. The suppression of instincts results in mental conflict and undesirable emotional tension. Hence, a more healthy way of dealing with the instincts should be employed in schools.
d. To appeal to instinct is a sound principle in all educational efforts.
e. The instinct combat is generally found at work in classroom rivalry and games. Students can be urged to destroy social evils, removal of illiteracy from the society etc.
f. In modern educational psychology, every possible effort is made to base the educational of the child on its instincts. Modern education aims at the excitation of one or the other instinct in a child in order to make any an every kind of education, natural as well as normal.

EMOTION

CONCEPT

An emotion is a complex feeling of mental agitation usually related with pleasure or pain which is excited by some idea or percept and accompanied by its characteristic bodily expression and strengthened by organic sensation.

The word ***'Emotion'*** is derived from the Latin word ***'Emovere'*** which literally means the stirred up or the excited state of the organism (body and mind). The emotional state, therefore, is marked by physiological changes. In emotional stage, the individual experiencing the emotional state passes through three stages — tension, release, and overt response.

Woodworth defines emotion in terms of stirred up state of the organism of the individual, which causes psychological and bodily changes and this provokes him to behave the way he behaves. An emotion is an acute stimulation of the individual as a whole, psychological in origin involving behaviour conscious experience and visceral functioning.

DEFINITIONS

The following are some pivotal definitions of emotions:

1. **Mc. Daugal** regards emotion as a mode of experience that accompanies the working of an instinctive act.
2. In the words of **Crow and Crow**, an emotion is a dynamic internal adjustment that operates for the satisfaction, protection, and welfare of the individual.
3. **Valentine** is of the opinion that when feelings become intense we have emotion.
4. According to James Dreamer, "It is a complex state of the organism, involving bodily changes of a widespread character – in breathing, pulse etc. and on the mental side, a state of excitement and usually an impulse towards a definite form of behaviour."

CHARACTERISTICS OF EMOTIONS

Analysis of the definition given by Young and others give us the following characteristics of emotions:

1. Emotional experience involves feeling such as anger, fear or joy.
2. Emotions are psychological in nature.
3. An emotional reaction includes an impulse towards some kind of action.
4. Emotion involves awareness or perception of what it is or what it might be, that causes the impulses and feelings.

FUNCTIONS OF EMOTIONS IN LIFE

Emotions play a very significant role in our life. Below we are explaining how it functions in human life –

1. **Emotions and physical health:** Physical health is greatly affected by emotions. In case of anger, and fear, our digestion is affected. It is fear which causes nervousness and confusion. Love and joy or happiness accelerate digestion and promote health.
2. **Speech:** Prolonged emotional strain may cause stammering. The cause of stammering of children is caused from emotional condition.
3. **Attitude of timidity or of aggression:** It may result from an emotional strain or from frustration in life.
4. **Learning:** Pleasant emotions motivate learning. It is said that nothing succeeds like success. One feeling of achievement gives rise to stimulation for better work in future. Thus, emotional distress and frustration interfere with learning efficiency.

HOW EMOTION CAN BE TRAINED?

Emotions are the central aspect of instincts. Therefore, the principles of redirection, sublimation, inhibition etc. also go a long way to modify the emotions. Emotions ought to be trained for various reasons. Extreme emotional outburst injures the personality of the child. It disturbs the mental equilibrium of the individual.

The control of emotions through the method of repression is very harmful. Psycho analysists have made a detailed analysis of the various neuroses that are caused from repressions. The best method of controlling emotions are to prevent the occasions, and opportunities that excite emotions.

THEORIES OF EMOTION

The theory of emotions attempts to relate the stimulus situation, to set the organic state and the bodily sensations. The James Lange theory of instinct is most popular theory of emotion. This theory was developed by William James and Card Lange. According to this theory, the emotional feelings consists of the mass of sensations coming from the body, specially the internal organs.

JAMES HAS ADVANCED THE FOLLOWING ARGUMENTS IN SUPPORT OF HIS THEORY

Organic disturbances produce certain emotions. Disorders of liver produce gloominess and irritability. In pathological cases of "objectless emotions", it is the pathological condition of the organism that produces emotions. The insane persons display different emotions which are unmotivated. These objectless emotions are produced by organic conditions.

CRITICISM OF JAMES-LANGE THEORY

The James-Lange Theory has been criticized on the following grounds:

a. It is not true to say that emotion can be arrested by arresting the expressions. If the emotion is refused any expression, it will not die. It will, on the other hand, leave in us a characteristic mood which will subsequently burst on the slightest provocation.
b. James has ignored the cognitive aspect of an emotion and this is the cause of his confusion. The emotions are aroused when any of our instincts is satisfied or thwarted.

W.B. CANON-BARD THEORY OF EMOTION

W.B. Canon and Bard had conducted several experiments which were in the form of surgical operations performed upon dogs and cats.

Canon showed on series of tests that adenine has the same effect on the viscera as unpleasant emotions, viz., fear and anger.

ON THE BEHAVIOUR THEORY OF EMOTION

The Behaviour J.B. Watson is of the view that an emotion is a hereditary reaction involving profound changes in the bodily mechanism as a whole but particularly in the visceral and glandular systems. Watson denies consciousness.

Hence, he could not agree with the views of James or Cannon, who gave equal importance to conscious experience of emotions along with organic changes. Watson thinks emotions to be identical with organic changes.

RELATIONSHIP BETWEEN INSTINCT AND EMOTION

a. The relation between instinct and emotion can be better understood by noting their affinity as well as distinction.

b. The primary emotions, i.e. fear, anger, with their original expressions are also innate like the instincts.

c. Emotional expression and instinct often shade off into each other and it is very difficult to distinguish them. For example, the barking of a dog may be interpreted as the expressions of anger and also as an expression of the combative instinct.

d. What arouses an instinct produces at the same time an emotion also. Emotions mostly occur when some basic needs are obstructed, or challenged or satisfied. Fear, for example, is reaction associated with some expected danger.

e. Emotion also serves the organism in a helpful manner in the satisfaction of its basic need. It is this affinity which makes Mc. Dougal thinks that emotion is the core of an instinct.

39

Education and Social Change in India

ROLE OF EDUCATION IN MODERNIZATION

MODERNIZATION AND EDUCATION

The Education Commission of India under the Chairmanship of D.S. Kothari reiterated the education is the main instrument of modernization. It can bring about change in all fields of life and nation – social, cultural, economic, technological and industrial.

If Education is to be the instrument of national development it should be:

1. Related to productivity.
2. Strengthen social and national integration.
3. Consolidate democracy.
4. Build character by cultivating social, moral and spiritual values.

It is an effort to bring about radical changes in the economic bases, technological methods, industrial, social and organizational level, It is to bring less advanced nations on par with far advanced nations.

The process is to be viewed as all in all process and not as compartmentalized one.

MODERNIZATION IN THE INDIAN SCENARIO

1. India provides an excellent example of puzzlement and paradoxes.
2. Pockets of modernity set against vast hinterland.
3. Powerful thrusts of the modernizers are stalled by traditional structures.
4. Economic policies are not supported by social policies.
5. Gap between the elite and masses.
6. Little correspondence between lofty formulation of policies and preparation.

The Education Commission 1946-66 says the process of modernization will, therefore, be directly related to the pace of educational advance, lastly modernization is the direct result of educational efforts.

HIGHLIGHTING IMPLICATIONS OF MODERNIZATION FOR EDUCATION

1. Demands teaching and testing technology should be modernized in order to achieve better results.
2. Instructional technology should make use of advanced audio-visual aids, tape recorder, movies a broadcasting network, television, teaching machines etc.
3. Role of Teacher in modernization of India.
4. Produce skilled and competent citizens.
5. Should all superstitions, welcome science and technology.
6. Instill into youngsters the benefits of Modernization.
7. Bring faith in modernization. Creative, constructive & realistic outlook should also be developed.
8. Kit-based instruction for teaching science, language lab for teaching language.
9. Diffused system of expectation rewards.
10. Ascription versus achievement dilemma.
11. Gap between ideals as the activity. They should shake off all prejudices and blind beliefs.

Education and modernization are closely linked-location effectively assists modernization. Education prepares the necessary manpower, skilled personnel to occupy different positions in life who would contribute for the growth of national wealth, education is the key to open the doors of the modernization in various fields of nation's life like economic, industrial technological and social.

PIVOTAL INFLUENCE OF EDUCATION IN HUMAN RESOURCE DEVELOPMENT

Human resources are the capital of the country. They are the wealth of natures. Education can only make an individual grow and develop fully.

Kothari Education Commission report (1964-66) highlight the role of education in human resource development in this way, "One of the major programmes in natural reconstruction is the development of our human resources, and in this there can be no limit to the education to be provided".

According to National Policy on Education of 1986, "It should now be possible to further identify the nature wide effort in human resource development, with education playing its multi faceted rote".

The solvering points shows very clearly the role education can play in the development of human resource.

BRING AWARENESS AMONG THE MASSES

To bring awareness and attitudinal change among the masses. Making the masses aware if the importance of education, facilities available its utility in democratic set up of life and make better life.

TO PROVIDE KNOWLEDGE

Knowledge explosion is must today. Knowledgeful people can only make progress in his life up to date knowledge is necessary to make up business better and suitable for the competitive market and discharge his duties to the entire satisfaction of the concerned officers.

TO PROVIDE BASIC SKILLS

Basic skills can be acquired by a person through the process of education. This complement of education is necessary pre-condition for modernization and self-reliant economy.

DEVELOPMENT OF HIGHLY QUALIFIED MANPOWER

The contribution of education is to facilitate the development of highly qualified anpower and generation of knowledge through research and development activities.

CHANGE IN ATTITUDE

Attitude of the people may be positive or negative. Education helps in changing the attitude from unfavourable to favourable, it helps in making the social climate of the individual and society more conductive.

HELPS IN SOCIALIZATION

Education socializes the individuals. Social efficiency is must for every individual to live in the society. The formal education given in the class or in the school and informal education which is given outside or in the school and information education which is given outside socializes the learner.

RESEARCH AND DEVELOPMENT

It is a pivotal aspect of education for human resource development is research, and development activities. In an ideal situation, research and development would be integrated with the requirements of socio- economic policy thrusts in the country.

All the ideas of Human Research Development should be applied with the help of education to increase productivity and excellence in organizations.

SCHOOL AS AN AGENCY OF SOCIALIZATION

ROLE OF THE SCHOOL IN THE SOCIALIZATION OF THE CHILD

Socialization is nothing but, transmitting the norms do's and don'ts in a convincing way to the child and making him translate those into practice in order to make the child acceptable and a befitting, member of the group or a society in future he is going to become a member.

There are many types of socialization, namely, formal socialization, informal socialization, diffused socialization etc. since the school is a formal agency established by the government it is very much interested in only formal type of socialization. Informal socialization is the act of home and church and peer groups etc.

There are three theories of socialization namely, symbolic, Mechanical and international. Symbolic type is that which brings modification at mental level in attitudes. Mechanical socialization is that which brings changes only in the exhibited behaviour of the child. Both of these types happened to be partial and incomplete because one interested in attitudes and the other in the behaviour. International socialization is said to be the complete and perfect and desired on which brings changes correspondingly in attitudes and behaviours both at the same time.

CO-RELATIONSHIP BETWEEN CULTURE AND EDUCATION

Culture reflects the level of civilization that a particular society has attained and involves cultivations of customs, traditions, folklore rituals and mannerisms etc. According to **John Dewey**, culture is the cultivation and appreciations of ideals, values art and recreational practices. Rugg and withers define culture as the total life of people that goes on with these groups, what the people in a given society think believe desire for.

THE THREE ASPECTS THAT ARE CONSIDERED MOST IMPORTANT AND THAT ARE

1. The culture is the external surface civilization;
2. The social institutions of the people; and
3. Education is the modifications of behaviour in conformity with the cultural norms of the society.

According to **Dr. Sarvepally Radha Krishnan**, the Late President of India, 'Culture is the content of education. Education without culture was for him, as the body without soul. Education refers the culture and culture feeds the education. Thus, they too are mutually and intimately related. Education serves as an instrument for the transmissions of cultural heritage. A child lives the mush greater part of his time in the cut of school culture and is thus educated by it moral than by the school any educational programmer must take into its account the nature of culture in which the schools are found'.

EDUCATION HAS THREE SIGNIFICANT FUNCTIONS ABOUT THE CULTURE MEANT

1. Education for acculturation;
2. Education for the observation of culture; and
3. Education for the development of culture.

Every nation has its own heritage and cultural background. Thus, Indian culture has a rich past and present. Indian Education system, hence should serve the cause of Indian culture. The constitution of India, through its various provisions, has guaranteed it the preservation and conservation of culture. Not only that, even sub-cultural systems also have a right to demand due treatment from the government and people.

Indian culture has the following essential characteristics truthfulness, non-violence, secularist outlook, the spirit of tolerance, spiritualistic temper, unity in diversity live and let live principle, absence of immediate values, universal equality, universal liberty, empathy, fellow- feeling, co-operation, loyalty, patriotism, respect for the elders, etc. All these are to be transmitted through education from generation to the next generation.

VARIEGATED ASPECTS THAT BRING OVER MODERNIZATION

Modernization is a process, a movement from traditional or quasi traditional order to desired type of technology and associated forms of social structure, value orientation, motivation and norms.

Modernization involves not only the changes in The material culture of nation but also its belief system, value and a way life on the whole. It is a process of transformation of society, from its backward framework to a forward looking, progressing and prospering structural build up.

This process started long ago in the history of many nations. After World War-II it gained impetus. Modernization does not mean mere imitation of some advanced countries. It is a process which helps a nation to establish its own identity. At the same time a nation has to learn much from developed nations.

SOCIAL CHANGE

It implies change in the social structure and functions of the various units which form society. Social structure includes social institutions like family, marriage system, caste system, educational institutions, customs, languages, and dress and food habits.

CAUSES RESPONSIBLE FOR SOCIAL CHANGE

a. Change in the climate is the cause of the evolution and devolution of civilizations and culture.

b. Rise in the population brings down living styles and conditions of people like unemployment, beggary, crime etc.

c. Knowledge growth is another factor for social change. New scientific thoughts, philosophies and ideas take the people on the new path.

d. Religious and social reformers like Swami Dayanand, Swami Vivekananda made the people of India conscious of their social responsibility.

e. Changes are brought about through planning. Five year plans and annual plans are prepared to bring about systematic changes.

f. Westernization has influenced culture, living styles, values etc. of the Indian people especially during the British Rule.

g. Industrialization has given rise to crimes, drinking growth of slums, banks, roads, trade union activities etc.

h. Urbanization has led to continuous migration from rural areas to towns.

i. Hinduization attempts are made to popularize beliefs and customs etc.

j. Indianization in which people belonging to different faiths tend to identify themselves with Indian culture.

k. Political factors like the rise of communism, Fascism, Nazism, entirely changed the social structure of several societies.

l. The British rules introduced a new system of education which changed the etiquettes, habits and manner etc. of the several sections of Indian Society.

m. The effect of mass India is what we listen to the news of the world on raid, watch T.V. and spend our leisure in a different way to the people of fifty years ago.

EDUCATION AS A POWERFUL TOOL

It is universally accepted fact that education is accepted as very powerful tool to describe changes in the society. Kothari Education Commission has categorically mentioned it in its report. It brings desired modernity, scientific humanism, rational thinking, national consciousness, tempered with the international understanding; social mobility and all the above factors of social changes are only possible when education is gained by man.

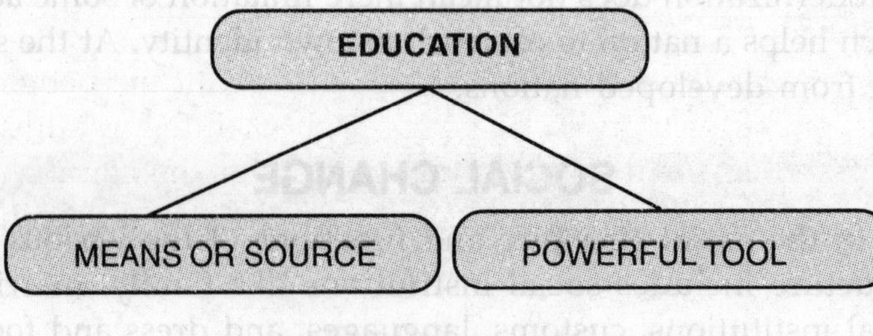

Fig. 11. Pivotal Skill of Education

EDUCATION AND DEVELOPED NATION

There is evidence in some of the developed nations that education brought changes. For e.g.. USA; USSR; Japan etc. hence, in India too there is no doubt, education would be able to brings changes in the Society. In order to do away traditionalism, casteism, classicism and untouchability differential treatment given to sex, narrow regionalism, communal tensions etc.

Education is the only way of overcoming all the above problems by bringing awareness towards the problems. Hence universal compulsory free primary education is introduced as a step in that direction under the constitutional provisions.

40

Education and Its Impact on National Integration

INTRODUCTION

National Integration means the feeling of oneness among all the people of the Nation. It is nothing but achievement of unity in diversity. Men of different faiths and creed live in India. Hence, it is essential for the unity and progress of the country that national and emotional integration should take place among people. After the Chinese and Pakistani aggression, its urgency has been more keenly felt. This work can be performed by the education.

EDUCATION FOR HUMAN CHARACTER

The aim of education is to build human character and to make young generation so able that they might assist in the achievement of democratic values. Such education would unite all people together. If people would be educated in a scientific way, they would rise above the political, economic, linguistic, religious and social differences in the interest of national integrity.

HUMAYUN KABIR WRITES

Nationhood does not depend on race language or religion or geography, singly or collectively, they all help, but on the feeling of belonging to one nation.

DEFINITION OF NATIONAL INTEGRATION

"National Integration is the includable prerequisite for fulfilment of our infant democracy and the consummation of our democracy is a matter which will be momentous consequence for the destiny of man having regard to the ancient history of our land and its size and its general importance in the scheme of things". **C.D. Deshmukh**

"National Integration cannot be built by brick and mortar or it can't be built by chisel and hammer. It has to grow silently in the minds and hearts of men. The only process is process of education".

S. Radhakrishnan

UNDERSTANDING OF NATIONAL INTEGRATION

One of the most urgent problems to be attended by the Nation in India is National Integration. The forces that ruled the country till 1947 from 1600 AD have introduced the disintegrating elements in all fields and at all levels of the Nation.

Unity in diversity : It is one of the lefties ideals of India respecting and appreciating the variety, we have to contemplate to attain unity. This is the philosophy, that teaches the secrecy of the nature. India's selection of the importance of unity in diversity and integration.

EDUCATION FOR DEVELOPMENT NATIONAL AND INTEGRATION UNDERSTANDING

India is a land of so many different religion, castes, creed, languages etc. one of the most difficult problem before us today is the building of a national mind by curbing the religious, linguistic and communal conflicts which tend to disunite us. The rise and fall of nation depends upon the extent of the development of the feelings of nationalism in its citizen. A nation uses education as a powerful means to achieve its desired ends and goals.

MERITS OF EDUCATION FOR NATIONAL INTEGRATION

1. Political Unity
2. Social Progress
3. Economic Progress
4. Development of Culture
5. Eradication of Corruption
6. Development of Self Sacrifice
7. Development of National Language

After Independence India facing a number of problems. The problem of national integration is a most serious one. To solve the problem we have to remove criticism, communalism, provincialism, political parties, diverse languages, social differences, lack of leadership and constant education, education for national integration is must for national development but it has own limitations and drawbacks.

CAUSES FOR DISINTEGRATED CONDITIONS

a. The local, regional, linguistic, case, communal and state loyalties.
b. Strikes, disregard for public property, disrespect and law and order, corruption in public life, communal clashes, student unrest etc.
c. Favouritism and corruption in public service.
d. Lack of good leadership in social, cultural education and political fields.
e. Lack of patriotism.

EDUCATION AS A MEAN OF NATIONAL INTEGRATION

Education is the best means for achieving the end of national integration. The system of education is considered not be conductive to posturing of national integration. In the texts books much material is found to be prejudicial to the posturing of national solidarity.

BASIC AIMS OF EDUCATION FOR NATIONAL INTEGRATION

The primary goal of education for national integration is the promotion of national unity by including in teachers and the taught the beliefs and conduct essential for democratic living in India.

The second aim of education for National Integration is to bring into conformity with democratic practices, the majority, minority groups conducts and relations.

The third aim is enable the educants and the educators to internalize.

CONCLUSION

India is the second largest country regarding to the Population in the world. India is a wonderland of diversified distinct religions and different castes, but now India's major problem all Indians have a sense of oneness and unity. National understanding means national citizenship and welfare of all citizens.

41

Education with Its Impact on International Understanding

INTRODUCTION

International understanding is an elusive term. Let us define it with the opinions of others. The true sense of international understanding is nothing apart from the 'Word Citizenship'. Goldsmith express the same idea when he says, "Internationalism is a feeling that the individual is not only a member of his State, but a citizen of the world.

EDUCATION AND INTERNATIONALISM

Above nationalism there is something more important and vital and that is internationalism. In order to fertilize this attitude or understanding, education should be adopted as a means of communication. Education enables a nation to have contacts and relations with the countries, and this contact ultimately results into international understanding and peace.

PRINCIPLES OF INTERNATIONAL UNDERSTANDING

a. The power of independent thinking should be cultivated in our youth and this principle should be at the base of international understanding.

b. Our dealings must be based on human principles.

c. If we want to equip our young men for international understanding we should train them for the practical use of the knowledge gained by them.

d. Teaching for international understanding is not the province of any one level of education.

CURRICULUM AND METHODS OF TEACHING FOR INTERNATIONAL UNDERSTANDING

a. In order to propagate ideal of international understanding, we must try to impart a right type of education to the students. A right type of education leads towards real knowledge and real understanding which has international bias.

b. The reorientation towards peace and understanding is only possible through right type of curriculum.
c. The world history enables us to understand the international relationship.

EDUCATION AND INTERNATIONAL COHESION

a. True democratic spirit should be developed.
b. Curriculum must be prepared in such a way as to develop an international attitude.
c. Exchange of youths and teachers between different nations is an important means to promote international understanding.
d. The concept of 'sovereign state' is a thing of the past nationalism and internationalism today are closely interdependent and a single state can hardly be self-sufficient in the economic, political and cultural fields.

EDUCATION WITH INTERNATIONAL UNDERSTANDING

One of the fundamental factors which stand against the growth of international cohesion is that almost every nation's educational programme emphasizes the principle of sovereign state. A child is taught to give the highest esteem to his own country. A healthy growth of international feeling can only be possible by a proper reform of the principles of education and its curriculum.

IN THE EARLIER YEARS OF EDUCATION, A CHILD SHOULD BE INCULCATED WITH THE FOLLOWING ASPECTS

a. The child should be taught the value of group participation. Fellowship always follows good will to others.
b. The child should regard the individual dignity of himself as well as others.
c. The education programme should by emphasis on interdependence of the nations.
d. The child should be taught to respect others and their views. He should show special attention to a man other caste, nationality or religion.

UNESCO AND INTERNATIONAL UNDERTSANDING

The UNESCO has laid down the following guidelines to the education for international understanding :

It should make clear that civilization results from contribution of many nations and that nations are interdependent.

It should explain the basic reasons for the difference in the modes of life of people, their customs, traditions and the means in which they have been resolved.

It should make clear that through ages moral, intellectual and technical progress of mankind tend to constitute a common heritage for all.

It should encourage the growth of healthy social outlook among children and thus pave the way to a better international understanding.

It should aim for a world-community and to create a world-society.

CONCLUSION

True democratic spirit should be developed. The students should be taught the essential principle of democracy, viz., to regard the rights and interests of others which must develop on international outlook.

Curriculum must be prepared in such a way as to develop an international attitude. Suitable text books are to be prescribed so as to acquaint the pupils of our country with the best national features of other countries.

42

Educational Technology

EDUCATIONAL TECHNOLOGY

As an instrument of work engaging human energies in a manner far surpassing the lure of war, as a Social dissolvent and read jester, and a philosophy of action, technology must be brought into the main stream of history. If the course of history is to be surveyed correctly and "*the dark imminence of the unknown future is to be in any way pen plated.*"

– Charls A Bead (1932)

What is Technology?

Technology is a scientific way for developing new techniques. It is a systematic way of evolving and applying these techniques. Technology can also be called a methodology for designing new techniques.

What is Educational Technology?

a. Educational technology is a process which can help the individual in making decisions and participating in many activities of society.

b. Educational technology is a communicative process which directly concerns with development, application and evaluation of systems, techniques and aids.

c. Educational technology is a method of improvement in human learning which is conceived with science of techniques, methods and media by which educational good can be realized.

d. Educational technology is described in an absolutely different way in it Dieuzede in the series B (opinion no. 30 international commission on the development of education, UNESCO)

Educational technology has to be seen as part of a persistent and complex endeavour of bringing pupils, teachers and technical means together in an effective way. Educational technology is not a bag of mechanical pricks, but, the organized design and implementation of learning systems taking advantages of but not expecting miracles from modern communications methods, visual aids, classroom organization and teaching method.

EDUCATIONAL TECHNOLOGY IN THE THEORY OF EDUCATION

Educational technology is a separate field dealing with the theory of education, with development and application of the educational resources which implies following principles:

a. Clarifies educational objectives.
b. Placing content of element in a logical order.
c. Specifies the process of teaching-learning.
d. Acquires the knowledge through development mode teaching.

THE FONTANA DICTIONARY OF MODERN THOUGHTS - U K 1978 STATES

Educational technology is the organization designed and implementation of learning systems taking advantages of but not expecting miracles from modern communications methods, visual aid, classroom organization and teaching methods.

AIMS OF EDUCATIONAL TECHNOLOGY

Technology is opium of intellectuals and for guarding against super egoism; the responsible technology is much more required.

The Educational Commission (1964-66) has recommended that the fundamental objectives in the curriculum should be improved so that teachers can be prepared for various responsibilities towards education.

MAIN OBJECTIVES OF EDUCATIONAL TECHNOLOGY

a. The major objectives of educational technology should be improved in all teachings learning process.
b. To determine the goals and formulate the objectives in behavioural terms.
c. To analyze the characteristic of learners.
d. To organize the content in logical or psychological sequence.
e. To mediate between content and resources of presentation.
f. To evaluate the learners performance in terms of achieving educational objectives.
g. To provide the feedback among other components for the modification of learners.

EDUCATIONAL TECHNOLOGY - ITS SCOPE

a. Educational technology is a process-oriented technique.
b. Educational technology is not limited to teaching and learning process and theories still teaching-learning process is influenced much more by educational technology.
c. If the educational technology is limited to audiovisual aids, mechanical and electronic area, the scope of educational technology becomes limited.

EDUCATIONAL TECHNOLOGY - ITS IMPORTANCE

HIGHLIGHTING IMPORTANCE OF EDUCATIONAL TECHNOLOGY IN THE AREA OF EDUCATION IS AS FOLLOW

a. Educational technology improves the teaching learning process and makes it more effective and process-oriented as well.

b. Educational technology has not only maintained the standard of education but also improved the ways of teaching by giving it teaching aids and programmed instructional material.

c. Mechanism of feedback devices for modification of teaching-learning behaviour can produce effective teachers in training schools.

Students appearing in the higher examination or competitive examinations may be benefited by organized educational programme on television and radio.

IMPORTANCE OF EDUCATIONAL TECHNOLOGY

Highlighting the Educational System is really concerned absolutely system revolutionized by Educational Technology. Educational system cannot go systematically without the help of educational technology. Every aspect of educational system is fully enlightened with educational technology. It has great importance in the educational field.

HIGHLIGHTING IMPORTANCE

The vital importance of educational technology in the arena of education is as under:

1. Educational technology improves the teaching-learning process and makes it more effective and process-oriented as well.
2. Electronic and mechanical gadgets which a common man possesses can be used for educational equipments.
3. Educational technology has not only maintained the standard of education but also improved the ways of teaching by giving it teaching aids and programmed instructional material.
4. Television, Radio, V.C.R., Computers and Internets can enrich as well as effect very much the education. Television, Radio, Tape-recorder and programmed instruction can also do wonders in the field of distance and correspondence learning.
5. Structure as well as nature of teaching can be developed and enriched with the help of educational technology.
6. Educational technology provides practices and strategies for reducing individual differences or strategies and practices which help teachers to teach according to individual differences of the learners.

Education in today's concern cannot go without the help of educational technology. The innovations of technology in the field of education have done wonders to educational process. It has not only maintained the structure but also improved the nature of educational process.

SELF-INSTRUCTIONAL TECHNOLOGY

a. Self-Instructional technique is a device in the science of learning. Since, **Prof. Skinner** introduced the term of teaching machine, this device has emerged as a revolutionary device of learning.
b. During the last decade self-instructional movement has attracted the attention of psychologists and educationists in different ways.
c. Self-Instructional technology is an approach to individualized instruction. But, it is an effective device to educate the masses.
d. Self-Instructional Technology has two approaches, one is 'Mass approach' and the other is 'individual approach'.

IMPORTANCE OF SELF-INSTRUCTIONAL TECHNOLOGY

a. Self-Instruction builds up a sequence of the content and it involves students' active participation. A learner is also a thinker.
b. Self-Instructional technique gives us the programming of material in order to teach the pupil to think. It is essentially based on a tutor-pupil relationship.
c. At present, in our conventional system of education there is emphasis on teacher class relationship. In this approach the learning is the result of the interaction between a programmed material and a student. It provides the student with as much practice quickly and the slowly learner to learn slowly. Hence, it is constructed on the pattern of the learning speed of the individual student.
d. Self-Instructional technique enables the learner to proceed at his own pace. It emphasizes programming of the subject matter. Programmed material is a sort of inanimate teacher purported to work as human teacher. Programmed material is sometime taken as a text-book.
e. It is one-side view of programmed material. It can no doubt, be compared with text-books in relation to subject matter but it goes beyond text book in the sense that it assumes the responsibilities of producing in a student a definite predictable set of behaviour.
f. This technology can be used fruitfully in home study also. It can save much time of the teacher who is often tried of the correction work of the individual student.

TYPES OF EDUCATIONAL TECHNOLOGY

It is suggested by Lumsdaine that there are three types of Educational Technology, namely

1. Educational Technology I or the Hardware Approach.
2. Educational Technology II or the Software Approach.
3. Educational Technology III or the System Approach

THE EXPLANATION

EDUCATIONAL TECHNOLOGY - I OR THE HARDWARE APPROACH

In educational technology hardware approach means the application of the principles of physical sciences and engineering to educational equipment, i.e. the deployment of audiovisual aids for the purpose of education. In other words we can say that Hardware approach has physical science and applied engineering as its basis.

In fact, without being aware of educational technology which happens to be recent discipline, teachers all over the world are using audio - visual aids to improve their teaching techniques.

EDUCATIONAL TECHNOLOGY - II OR THE SOFTWARE APPROACH

In software approach, the basis of all thinking and working is behavioural science and psychology of learning. The teacher with added knowledge of software approach can use the films, fish-cards, tapes etc. for various purposes. There is no end to his thinking. He can plan better teaching which results into better learning.

Software approach uses the principles of psychology for the purpose of behaviour modification. It makes use of verbal process. It is application of teaching-learning process that are being made use of.

EDUCATIONAL TECHNOLOGY - III OR THE SYSTEM APPROACH

The third type of educational technology is said to be system approach. Computer science is the basis of this approach which is systematizing everything of the complicated teaching-learning process. In this approach, the input and output along with the strategies being used are evaluated.

MERITS AND DEMERITS OF EDUCATIONAL TECHNOLOGY

THE MERITS OF EDUCATIONAL TECHNOLOGY IN THE FIELD OF EDUCATION CAN BE MAINTAINED IN THE FOLLOWING WAY

a. It is educational technology which provides clear cut information and knowledge to the teacher.
b. The teachers are able to learn new to prepare modules, Programmed learning materials.
c. The teachers become more efficient academically professionally and technologically.
d. In the discharge of classroom duties, the teachers are able to handle their techniques more confidently.

DEMERITS OF EDUCATIONAL TECHNOLOGY

a. Proper use of educational technology requires sincerity, dedication and determination.
b. More trained and efficient man-power is required to handle the different aspects of educational technology.
c. Educational technology requires a lot of time for its successful implementation.
d. We cannot properly use educational technology where there are minimum infrastructural facilities on the educational institution.

43

Educational Sociology

MEANING

Meaning of Educational Sociology is such a branch of sociology which has come into existence as a synthesis between **"Education"** and **"Sociology"**. It studies all social processes and social interactions for social development and welfare without when the nature and problems of education cannot be solved.

The term **'Sociology'** consists of two words of society – 'Socio' a Latin word which mean 'companion' or 'associate' and 'logos' means 'study' or 'science'. Thus, Sociology literally means, the study of Society.

"Educational sociology is the study of interaction of the individual and his cultural environment". **Brown**

"Educational sociology is the scientific study of the relationship between education and society". **Ottaway**

Educational sociology is the scientific study of how people live in social groups especially including the study of education that is obtained by the living the social groups, and education that is needed by the member to live efficiently in social groups.

AIMS AND EDUCATIONAL SOCIOLOGY

a. To study the prevailing social condition.
b. To acquire knowledge about school work and the work of teachers in relation to society and social progress.
c. To study the social factors and their effects on the individual.
d. To study the effects of social elements on the school.
e. To make the person a useful citizen, a person with social and rational feeling.
f. To construct a curriculum of education with full understanding of the economic and cultural tendencies of society.

g. To help the individual lesson how to use the leisure time properly.
h. To gain knowledge about democratic ideologies.
i. To employ research techniques for achieving the aims of educational sociology.

SCOPE OF EDUCATIONAL SOCIOLOGY

Educational Sociology is ever growing and advancing subject. Brown depicts the field of educational sociology through the following:

a. Field of Educational Sociology.
b. Individual - His world of people and things.
c. Interaction.

1. Educational sociology is wide and comprehensive subject; it studies the effect of social interaction on education and of education on social interaction.
2. Educational sociology is to discover the area of interaction within the family and then in school & other agencies of sociology.
3. Educational sociology is related to educational psychology. Both of them deal with the school as the agency of education. Both seek to determine and influence the school's effect upon individual behaviour.
4. There is constant interaction between the individual and his cultural environment which are dynamic. They change due to the impact knowledge explosion.
5. Educational sociology is a means of social progress. It eliminates ills and establishes good social customs. It helps in making the environment dynamic.
6. One of the factors of study of educational sociology is mutual relation of teachers and students.
7. The place of a teacher in society will be considered.
8. Educational sociology studies the progress of democratic feelings in school.

The scope of Educational Sociology covers those aspects of sociology which are applicable in the field of education and enable us to understand the child from the point of view of total social milieu. Thus, the scope of educational sociology is very wide and these may be pointed out as below:

a. Contacts between local social institution and educational institutions.
b. Effect of social life on individual and educational institutions.
c. Relationship between teacher and student.
d. Suitable changes in the curriculum for the development of the individual as well as the society.
e. Evaluation of different programmes of press, radio, films etc. in the social activity.
f. It also studies how various social agencies like school, home, religious institutions, the play group etc. help in the transmission of culture.
g. It studies how the socialization of the child takes place as a result of social interaction involving competition, conflict, cooperation with other members of the society.

i. It studies the impact of sociological thinking on various aspects of education, i.e. aims of education, curriculum and social organization.

j. It examines how education can serve as a means of bringing about change and can enable the child to have social control.

SOCIALIZATION

Man is a social animal and he cannot live alone. At the time of birth, the child knows nothing. But, gradually he comes to understand the relationship between itself and the other person. Every society prescribes its own ways and means of giving social training to its new born members so that they may develop their own personality. This social training is called **'Socialization'.**

According to **Mac Iver,** "*Socialization is the process by which social beings establish wider and profounder relationships with one an other, in which they become more bound up with and more dependent on one another, in which they develop the sense of their obligation and responsibility towards others, in which they grow more perceptive of the personality for themselves and of others and build up the complex structure of nearer and wider associations*".

FACTORS AFFECTING SOCIALIZATION

There are four factors that affect socialization. These are - imitation, suggestion, identification and language.

Imitation: Imitation means copying by an individual of the actions of another. It is the main factor in the process of socialization of the child.

Suggestion: It is the process of communicating information which has no logical or self evident basis. Propaganda and advertising are based on the fundamental psychological principles of suggestion.

Identification: The child cannot make any distinction between his organism and environment. Most of his actions are random. These are natural reactions of which is not conscious.

Language: Language is the medium of social inter-course or interaction. It is the means of cultural transmission.

Environment: It plays an important role in the process of socialization. Those children who get healthy environment and surroundings get soon socialized and pick up good manners and habits as compared with the children who do not get good environment. It is due to environment that one becomes either social or anti-social.

RELATIONSHIP BETWEEN EDUCATION AND SOCIOLOGY

A society is a group of organized individuals. It is society which provides the individual with basic security. The individual is encouraged to play his role in terms of his potentialities and achievements.

ACCORDING TO MAC IVER AND PAGE

According to Mac Iver and Page, man is dependent on society for protection, comfort, nature, education, equipment, opportunity and the multitude of definite services which society provides. He is dependent on society for the content of his thoughts, dreams and aspirations.

THE IMPORTANT RELATIONSHIP

The relationship between education and sociology is well understood from the following points:

a. It is sociology which develops laws and principles which are adopted by the educational system for its improvement.
b. Sociology has contributed much to the planning, organizing, executing and evaluating the educative process.
c. Sociology develops methods and techniques to be utilized by the educational system to bring about the desired behavioural and attitudinal changes.
d. Sociology is the science of society and education is an implicit aspect of any social system.

AGENCIES OF EDUCATION

Various agencies play their role in socializing the child. These are

Educational Institutions: The educational institutions such as schools and colleges are considered as important agencies of socializing the child.

Social Institutions: Social Institutions are considered as important agencies socialization of the child. These institutions have an impact on the social development of the child.

Neighbourhood: It is from the neighbourhood that the child learns about the social values, and the ways of living with others.

Family or Home: The most important role played by the home or family is the process of socialization. It is considered as the primary group which brings about socialization in the child. The child's first social development takes place in the family.

Play Group: Play group plays vital place in socializing the child. As the child grows up, he gradually goes out of the house and comes in contact with other children, and form the play group.

Religious Institutions: Religious institutions or organizations like Temples, Churches, Mosques, Gurudwaras etc. influence the process of socialization to a great extent. These organizations are considered as primary social institutions.

Language: Language is a medium of communication or interaction with other members of the society. Language, in many ways, is the most fundamental factor in bringing about the process of socialization.

Mass-Media: Mass-media are the most effective instrument of the socialization process. Newspapers, Magazines, Radio, Cinema, Television, and Computer etc. are the carrier of different types of knowledge and news to the individual and society.

44

Curriculum and Development

CURRICULUM

Curriculum in a broad sense is inclusive of complete school environment and can hope to achieve much more in the development of the whole man than the narrow classroom curriculum. Curriculum includes all the learner's experiences in and outside school that are included in a programme which is devised to help him develop mentally, physically, emotionally, socially, spiritually, and morally.

DEFINITIONS

Following definitions throw light on the concept, meaning and scope of curriculum:

According to Edward A. King, "Curriculum includes all the learning experiences which children have under the direction of the school".

Harold Spears considers curriculum as "all the activities of children that are carried forward under the direction of the teacher".

PRINCIPLES OR DOCTRINES OF CURRICULUM CONSTRUCTION

The Secondary Education Commission (1952-53) that went into all aspects of secondary education in the context of educational needs of modern India suggested the following principles of curriculum construction. These principle, by and large, still hold good.

The Principle of Totality of Experiences: "*Curriculum*" says the Commission "*does not mean only the academic subjects traditionally taught in the school, but it includes the totality of experiences that pupil receives through the manifold activities that go on in the school, in the classroom, library, laboratory, play grounds and in the numerous informed contacts between teachers and pupils. In this case, the whole life of the school becomes the curriculum which can touch the life of the students at all points and help in the evolution of a balanced personality.*"

THE PRINCIPLES OF INTER-RELATIONSHIP OF SUBJECTS

The curriculum is a systematic group of subjects or courses required for graduation of certification. It is not a combination of a number of isolated uncoordinated watertight compartmentalization of subjects.

THE PRINCIPLE OF VARIETY AND ELASTICITY

Undeniably there are certain areas of knowledge, skill and appreciation which all students should learn. But they should be kept to the minimum.

THE PRINCIPLE OF COMPREHENSIVENESS

If curriculum has to satisfy different needs, interest and inclinations of students if it has adapted to individual differences, it must be comprehensive.

THE PRINCIPLE OF RELATIONSHIP WITH COMMUNITY LIFE

The modern tendency is towards a life-centered experience curriculum. The backbone of curriculum should be some productive work satisfying local needs and situations.

THE PRINCIPLE OF TRAINING FOR LEISURE

Curriculum should include not only activities and experiences leading to productive work, of it should provide experiences—social, artistic and aesthetic— that may make school life pleasant. Cultivation of different hobbies, for example, will be the best way of training for leisure.

THE PRINCIPLE OF BALANCE

School curriculum should maintain balance between various activities and experiences. It should have a balance between direct and indirect experiences liberal and professional education compulsory and optional subjects.

MODERNIZATION AND CURRICULUM

Curriculum is considered as an important tool in the hands of the educator to bring about necessary changes in the pupils. It, therefore, should be in accordance with the needs of the society.

Definitions and concepts of curriculum have changed radically during recent years. In earlier days, curriculum was regarded as a list of matter or a course of study which pupils were expected to learn. In those days, book learning was the only learning to be pursued. The text-book largely determined the curriculum.

CONCEPT OF A MODERN CURRICULUM

a. It strikes a balance between compulsory and optional subjects, between experiences promoting intellectual and physical growth. A balanced curriculum produces a balanced personality.
b. A modern curriculum caters to the needs of individual differences of children.

c. It stresses the creative aspects of the learning process.
d. It interrelates play and work.
e. It takes into account the development of values enshrined in our Constitution.
f. It helps in the development of knowledge, attitudes and skills needed in a socially efficient individual.

MEANING AND SIGNIFICANCE OF CURRICULUM

MEANING

Curriculum in a wide sense includes all the subjects, experiences and activities of the schools which are directed under the guidance of the teachers.

SIGNIFICANCE OF CURRICULUM

Curriculum is the most important tool in the hands of the school staff for the development of the whole child and his all-round development—emotional, ethical, intellectual, moral, physical and social. It is the life blood of the school. It serves as a suitable guide to the students and teachers.

VOCATIONAL CURRICULUM

The Vocationalized Spectrum or course or curriculum that is referred to embraces in the UNESCO language "*these aspects of the educational process involving, in addition to general education, the study of technologies and related sciences and the acquisition of practical skills, aptitudes, understanding and knowledge relating to occupations in the various sectors of economic and social life*".

THE VOCATIONALIZED COURSE PATTERN

The Adiseshiah Committee (1978) has recommended that the pattern of the course and the allocation of time for the Vocationalized Spectrum be –

	Course	Time Allocation
1.	Language (s)	15%
2.	General Foundation Course	15%
3.	Elective Vocational Subjects	70%

GENERAL FOUNDATION COURSE

The objectives or goals of the course are to enable the student to –

a. Become aware of the need for rural development and self-employment.
b. Understand the place of agriculture in the national economy.
c. Develop skills and managerial abilities to run small-scale and cottage industries.
d. Gain insight into the problems of unemployment, underemployment and economic backwardness of India.

ACTIVITY CURRICULUM

The present century is sometimes called the **'century of the child'.** Many educators would like to make him the **'monarch'** in the process of education. It is considered that **'learning by pupils'** is more important than **'teaching by the teacher'**.

RIGID AND FLEXIBLE (DIVERSIFIED) CURRICULUM

A rigid curriculum is a static curriculum also. It fails to take into account the individual differences of children and differences in the geographical, industrial and economic conditions of the regions.

SUBJECT-CENTERED CURRICULUM

A subject-centered curriculum is organized in such a way that the greatest emphasis is laid on facts, principles and skills in a subject.

The main assumption is that all children can learn at the same rate from the same source. An intelligently organized curriculum ensures a reasonably comprehensive or inclusive overview of the cultural heritage.

THE CHILD-CENTERED CURRICULUM

The most important defect of the subject centered curriculum ensure a reasonably comprehensive or inclusive overview of the cultural heritage.

CORE-CURRICULUM

Little agreement is found among people as to what constitutes a core. A somewhat plausible definition of core is given as under.

"The core curriculum includes learning experiences that are fundamental for all learners because they derive from our common individual drives or need and from our civic and social needs as participating members of a democratic society".

SUGGESTIONS FOR IMPROVEMENT IN CURRICULUM

The Education Commission (1964-65) made the following suggestions:

a. Curriculum should be made flexible.
b. Contents of the curriculum should be based on research.
c. Upto date and modern facts and trends should be taken into consideration while constructing the curriculum.
d. Advancements made in sciences and technology should be incorporated in the curriculum.

TERM OF CO-RELATION OF STUDIES

In simple and lucid words, co-relation of studies implies connecting knowledge of one subject with another subject or co-relating all subjects and knowledge to environment. Gandhiji's scheme of basic education lays emphasis on teachings of languages, history, geography, mathematics, science etc. with craft, physical and social environment so that whatever a child learns becomes integrated.

PSYCHOLOGICAL BASES OF CORRELATION

Herbart was the first educator to put forward the concept or idea of correlation of studies. He indicated that if something is to be taught to the child, efforts must be made to connect it with the previous knowledge possessed by the student.

PHILOSOPHICAL BASES OF CO-RELATION

The idea or concept of correlation is based on the philosophical principle that knowledge cannot be compartmentalized as it has an inherent unity or oneness. Knowledge comes a unit in the life outside the school and is never found separated in different objects or in different branches of the same subject.

FORMS OF CO-RELATION

Co-relation of studies may take 4 forms : (a) incidental, (b) systematic, (c) integration, (d) concentration.

Incidental correlation demands no previous planning on the part of the curriculum constructor. The teacher presents his material in a broad way and co-ordinates it with what pupils know in other subjects.

45

Education with Democracy

DEMOCRACY

History tells that common people have been suppressed for a very long period. Formerly, there were monarchical or aristocratic forms of government in almost all parts of the world. Monarchy and aristocracy has their own good administration. They also develop society.

Democracy arose in the west as a consequence of the revolution ideas of the great thinker Rousseau. Being impressed by the ideas of Rousseau common people wake up to the democratic ideals and decided to break the chain of slavery.

MEANING OF DEMOCRACY

We often use the word democracy in the political sense. From political point of view democratic government is based on the will of public. The famous words of **Abraham Lincoln** "Democracy is the government of the people, by the people and for the people'.

Politics is only one side of democracy its other side is economic democracy. All the people have a right to own property.

Social democracy is also a democracy. In social field, democracy would mean the absence of class differences, different sections of society castes and sub-castes create feeling of differences.

We see democracy is not only a method of administration but also a form of social system. In democracy every personality is important and every individual gets equal opportunity for the development of his personality.

DOCTRINES OF DEMOCRACY

Liberty, equality and justice are the basic principles of democracy. There seems to be a difference of opinions about the answer to the question- ***"Is equality possible ?"*** according to the famous philosopher, Santayana, the principle of equality itself is defective. He says

"Equality of un-equals is inequality: it cannot be equality.

Justice is also an important principle of democracy. What precisely does justice mean is, however, not an easy question to answer ?

'Just' implies **'right'** but both the terms are not synonyms. Similarity **'unjust'** implies **'wrong'** but is not synonymous with it.

Principle of Justice is linked up with the concept of equality. According to Hartmann the essential feature in justice is "The idea of equality; equal right, equal duty with others". We see that equality and justice are interrelated principles.

The degree to which equality is preached and praised is a measure of the economic progress over time. It seems that the problem of equality at its root is neither cultural nor political, but economic.

DEMOCRACY IN EDUCATION

Democracy education is different from the authoritarian type of education. Today, education and educationists are in favour of democratic education. The following modern trends in education can be easily termed as democratic –

a. Bondages of caste, creed and class in education are breaking.

b. Importance of child's personality is increasing.

c. Attention is being paid not only to child education but also to adult education. Every individual has to be educated. Adult literacy, adult education and social education are also being arranged.

d. The principle of equality of educational opportunities is attracting the attention of a education.

e. Great deal of liberty is being given to child in democratic education.

f. Attempts are being made to maxim curriculum broad elastic and suitable to the need of society.

g. Social principle have principles with special important in learning, therefore, social experiences must be given in the class.

h. The authority have started framing rules and regulations with the co-operation of student's so that they might happily accept them.

INDIAN DEMOCRACY

THE PREAMBLE TO THE CONSTITUTION INDICATE

We, the people of India having solemnly resolved to constitute India into a sovereign, socialistic, democratic republic and to secure to all its citizens.

Justice, social, economic and political; liberty of thought, expression, belief, faith and worship; equality of status and opportunity; and to promote among them all –

Fraternity, assuring the dignity of the individual and the unity of the nation; in our constituent assembly this 26th day of November, 1949, do here be adopt, enact and given to ourselves this constitution.

Basic principle of Indian democracy have been discuss well in a pamphlet entitled, **'we and our country'** issued by government of India. It will not be out of place to discuss some of such principles here.

Social justice seeks to secure for every individual his rightful place in the society free from handicaps that social traditions may have produce by uses and custom untouchability is abolished and its practice forbidden.

The concept of economic justice requires that citizens shall have the right to acquire hole and enjoy properly and practice any profession or occupation or trade of their choice.

No religious instructions shall be provided in educational institutions maintained out of state funds. Every persons has a right preserved any distinct manner or culture of his own. For this training of leadership is necessary.

EDUCATION AND NATIONAL OBJECTIVES

TO INCREASE THE PRODUCTIVITY

It can be done in four ways - Firstly, education should become part of all courses at all the stages of education. Secondly, work experience should be related to technology and industrialization. Finally, Secondary Education should be Vocationalized and at higher education level technical and agricultural education should receive emphasis.

TO ACHIEVE SOCIAL AND NATIONAL INTEGRATION

The commission has taken a note of the growth of local, regional, linguistic and state loyalties in India and holds that the achievement of social and national integration is an important objective of education.

TO ACCELERATE THE PROCESS OF MODERNIZATION

Modern society is based on technology education has to develop proper interest, skills, attitudes and values so that the pace of modernization may accelerated.

TO CULTIVATE SOCIAL, MORAL AND SPIRITUAL VALUES

The commission has suggested that education should also aim to cultivating proper values in the students.

The commission has also suggested that a tolerant study of all religions should also be promoted ours is a multi-religious society.

AIMS OF DEMOCRATIC EDUCATION

Aims of democratic education have been discussed in many ways. Secondary education commission has decided some aims of education by analyzing the educational needs of Indian Democracy. According to the commission following are the aims of democratic education:

DEVELOPMENT OF DEMOCRATIC CITIZENSHIP

It is necessary for the success of democracy that every citizen should love democracy. We have to develop intellectual awakening and free thinking in children.

EDUCATION FOR THE ART OF LIVING

In a democratic society, every individual is significant. Individual has to be trained in the art of leading community life. The art of living cannot be learned without suitable education and experience. Progress of society is possible only by mutual to co-operation of people.

DEVELOPMENT OF A SENSE OF TRUE PATRIOTISM

True patriotism is another important aim which the education has foster. In a very real sense, therefore, 'Patriotism is not enough' and it must be supplemented by a lively realization of the fact that we are all members of one world.

DEVELOPMENT OF PERSONALITY

There are several factors of personality. There should be an all round development of personality. In modern school attention is paid only to intellectual development.

EDUCATION FOR LEADERSHIP

Narrow minded leaders cannot make progress in the field of politics, science, literature; art etc. meaning of leadership should be confined only to political leadership. In all fields leadership should be there. For this training of leadership is necessary.

46

Culture and Cultural Lag

CONCEPT OF CULTURE

Culture is a very broad item which is interpreted differently by different people. Some people regard culture as a universal attitude to life, and some people accept it as a way of living and talking etc.

Culture has been defined in a number of ways. The most accepted meaning of culture is that it is the total way of life. In its broad meaning it covers man's material civilization like tools, weapons, clothing, shelter, machines, buildings, industrial products, as well as non-material civilization like language, literature, art morality, law and government.

CULTURE – DEFINED

Culture is the way of life of a group of people in a closed society. E. B. Tylor says culture is that complex whole which includes knowledge, belief, art, morals, laws, custom and any other capabilities and habits acquired by a man as a member of society.

a. H. Rugg's view on culture means the total life of the people that goes on with these groups; what the people in a given society to think, feel, believe, desire, fear.

b. Ellwood's definition suggest two aspects of culture non-material (aesthetic, intellectual and spiritual) and material (tools, weapons, building, clothing and shelter)

Culture is the outcome of social interaction. It is a social heredity. It is an instrument of growth.

CHARACTERISTIC FEATURES OF CULTURE

Complex whole : Culture is a complex whole processing some kind of unity.

Psychological achievement : Culture embraces an array of psychological achievement it is due expressed of external and mental life.

Material objects : Culture includes material objects is those of art of morality.

A Reality : Culture has its reality. It is good if it has some utility to the individual as well as society.

Obtained by living in Society : Culture is obtained by living in a society. Cultural traits and patterns are transmitted from one generation to another.

Process of Change : Culture is dynamic, not static, it is in constant change. The changing condition bring about changes is culture. It ought to be sensitive to the changing situations.

A Characteristic Pattern : It exhibits a characteristic pattern associated with any permanent need in social life. For example - spoon, fork, and knife are used for eating food by English, hand and fingers by Indians.

Culture has quality of diffusion and assimilation. It leads to the progress of the society.

Culture has quality to purify unwanted traits.

Culture is man-made.

Culture controls people : It meets recurring demands of mankind. "Civilization is used in association with culture".

SUB-CULTURE

The very form of culture is very extensive and the world is so large that all its population cannot come into contact with each other at a time. Different societies are affected differently by different faiths and beliefs, custom, traditions, ideas, spiritual and spiritual process. Such a environment is called the culture of that Society, group or nation. This is not the wider form of Culture, but, it is its narrow form which may be a sub-culture. Such sub-cultures are found in several nations, communities and tribes. This is the narrow form of universal culture.

WHY CULTURE?

Culture is fully needed, because, different elements and things included in it fulfil human needs in one form or the other.

a. Each person is influenced by his geographical environment. Hence, every person has to take up the help of culture in the natural environment around him.
b. Man generally adopts variegated ways and means for his social adjustment here, he tries to establish good relations with other members of the entire society.
c. The capability and the personality of man is developed by his efforts of adaptation in the natural and social environment.

CULTURAL LAG

Cultural lag is defined as the degree to which certain goals and aspects of culture lag behind the changes in its other aspects. Hence, all the aspects of our modern culture don't change at the same rate.

In our present society, economic system is changing fast; industrial economy is replacing the rural economy. Hence, the religion and social goals are not keeping Peace with the economic aspects.

47

Education and Globalization

CONCEPT – GLOBALIZATION

The term 'Globalization' means integration of economics and societies through cross-country flows of information, ideas, technologies, goods, service, capital, finance and people. It deals with the interdependent world economy.

GLOBALIZATION DEFINED

a. Globalization is defined as "*the growing economic interdependence of countries worldwide through increasing volume and variety of cross-border transaction in goods and services and of international capital flows and also through the more rapid and widespread diffusion of technology*".

b. Globalization deals with interdependent world economy dealing with globalization of markets and productions.

FACTORS CONTRIBUTING TO GLOBALIZATION

a. Widening markets and increase in market size with companies market within and outside the country.

b. Surplus resources and optimum utilization of their surplus.

c. Facilitating a company from a recession bit economy in another country.

d. Firms access to larger markets enabling them to take greater advantage economics of scale resulting in cheap and better quality products.

e. Consumers also gain as they access to greater of products in the form of lower priced and better quality products as a results of increased competition.

f. The principle of division of labour is an overriding benefit contributing to globalization. It increases world output and raises the material standard of living.

GLOBALIZATION AND EDUCATION

The increased development of a global market (Globalization) with improved communications links throughout the world, increase global competition and increase similarity of tastes in reducing the differences between internal and international trade. Under the provision of General Agreement on Trade Services (GATS), Indian education is bound to face formidable competition from the foreign players.

These days we find a number of foreign universities and colleges are making intensive efforts to enhance their presence in India by offering allotting packages of academic programmes.

To check the globalization of education process, the All India Council for Technical Education (AICTE) has decided to regulate the entry of foreign universities into India, and restrict to start a programme its approval collaborate with an AICTE approved college.

CONCLUSION

Globalization of education on one side may appear to transmit culture. This may result in homogenization of the society. Globalization of education to economists lead to international trading of education and remove the community feelings and bring the whole world under one roof.

48

Educational Planning

EDUCATIONAL PLANNING - CONCEPT

a. The concept of educational planning has been recently developed.
b. It is necessary to poor experiences of various countries in planning and evolve a suitable technique of planning and evaluation.
c. The UNESCO has organized some conferences and seminars on educational planning on regional basis in recent years.
d. It has also published some valuable literature on the subject and arranged to send experts and train personal required for the purpose.

EDUCATIONAL PLANNING - DEFINED

"Educational planning is the exercising of foresight in determining the policy, priorities and costs of an educational system, having due regard for economic and political realities for the systems potential for growth, and for the needs of the country and of the pupils served by the system".

OBJECTIVES OF EDUCATIONAL PLANNING

a. Quantitative planning which refers to the school population, enrolment, dropouts, teaching and supervisory personnel, buildings, laboratories, equipment, furniture, teacher pupil ratio, unit costs. etc.
b. Qualitative planning which concerns aims, structure, curricula, research etc.
c. Administrative planning which deals with administration at all levels, personnel etc.
d. Financial planning which deals with costs, income, expenditure, grants etc.

PHASES OF PLANNING

1. Single value forecasting stage.

2. Internal dynamics, in order to know it, analysis techniques are used.
3. Attempt in order to economize attempts.
4. Planning is a process stage. It includes
   a. Definition of objectives :
   b. Design of strategy of plan to need the objectives.
   c. Estimate or resource requirements supplementation.
   d. Evaluation.
5. Continuous approach process to be treated as a continuous process.

TYPES OF EDUCATIONAL PLANNING

Educational planning is done on the basis of its targets. The plans are of different types here we shall discuss some of the major types of educational plans.

OVERALL PLANNING

Overall planning of education involves application on co-ordination of social research methods and of principles and techniques of education administration economic and finance with the participation and support of general public in education for the people with definite aims.

TYPES OF PLANNING BASED ON GEOGRAPHICAL EXTENT

In this kind of planning geographical extent is pointed out by the nature of planning itself. They are mainly of the following types:

a. National Planning - Covering the entire country
b. Regional Planning - Based on different regions, state plans come in this category.
c. District Planning - Planning is done at district level.
d. Institutional Planning - Planning is done in the entire institutions.

TYPES BASED ON COVERAGE

This means any plan is based on a level of education. A stage of education or all stages of education are covered on this basis two types of planning is done. They are

COMPREHENSIVE PLANNING

In this type of planning whole country is covered including all stages of education like primary, secondary and university stages, it is also known as integrated planning.

SECTOR PLANNING

This type of planning is based on ne sector of education like primary education, university education, of women, education for deprived. Adult education are planned in sector planning.

TYPES BASED ON DURATION

When the planning is done on the basis of duration it is of different type. Here time frame is important. They are the following:

ANNUAL PLANNING

Planning is done for one year. It is yearly planning is done.

SHORT TERM PLANNING

When planning is done for about 4 years or more it is short term planning generally the minimum limit of years is 8 years. Our five year plans come under this category.

LONG TERM PLANNING

Generally in this kind of planning the duration is from 15 to 30 years. Very few countries adopt this type of planning.

TYPES BASED ON APPROACH

This type is based on method or model or approach to planning. This is of 3 types which are following:

MODEL ORIENTED APPROACH

This planning is done on the model of planning system of some country. Many countries accept England, U.S.A., Russia, or France as models.

NEED BASED APPROACH

Based on the Social needs, national traditions and social aspirations of the people.

RESOURCE BASED APPROACH

In this type of planning we have to estimate the resources of the society or country first and thereafter we have to plan education according to these resources.

ADDITIONAL TYPES

There are some other types of planning which we referred to sometimes we talk of these types in our planning. They are the following –

QUALITATIVE PLANNING

Web in planning we are much more concerned about number of chairs, tables, black boards, buildings, enrolment, teachers, students etc. we say it is qualitative planning.

QUANTITATIVE PLANNING

In it the aims of education, curriculum, co-curricular activities, teacher education, guidance counseling, and researcher are taken into account while planning.

ADMINISTRATIVE PLANNING

It is concerned about the planning according to needs of educational administration at primary, secondary or college level of education.

ECONOMIC PLANNING

It is concerned about economic issues like income, expenditures, shops, endowment etc.

URBAN PLANNING

Planning about education in schools and colleges run by corporation and municipalities.

RURAL PLANNING

It is easier to plan about urban schools but it is very difficult to plan about a school or college in a rural area.

POWER PLANNING

Economists have been saying that people are an important part of the National wealth, measured by that labour contributes to output; the productive capacity of human beings is now vastly larger than all other forms of wealth taken together.

MAN POWER PLANNING

The choices have to be made when resources are limited. And as soon as we talk about choices, the idea of some sort of planning flashes in the mind and that planning certainly may be called the Man Power Planning in relation to education.

It is now broadly accepted that education is corrected with economic growth mainly this connection has three aspects. The first is the supply skilled manpower.

MICRO PLANNING

Micro Planning is different from Macro Planning which takes into account the country as a unit. In macro planning the income and expenditure of the country as a whole, the budget of India, the inflation rate, growth rate of the nation as a unit are considered.

49

Institutional Planning

INTRODUCTION

An institutional plan is a set of programmes prepared by an educational institution on the basis of its felt-needs and the knowledge of its resources available and likely to be available with a view to improve the school standards and practices and with a view to provide for the future development of the institution.

MAIN FEATURES OF AN INSTITUTIONAL PLAN

Need Based

An institutional plan is prepared keeping in view the needs of the school as identified by the school staff.

Specificity

There cannot be a plan for all the institutions. The district education officer will not issue instructions which are mandatory for all the schools regarding the scope the content of the plan.

Policy of Optimum Utilization

The institutional plan is not expenditure oriented. The institution, while planning, does not mainly aim at preparing its financial requirements for any programme of improvement and development.

Augmenting Human Efforts

As a corollary to the maximum utilization of human resources, special features of the institutional plan will not only be the maximum utilization of human resources, but also a conscious attempt to augment the human effort which are so important for a large number of educational programmes which require imagination and thinking rather than finance and additional advantages.

Aim oriented

The entire plan at the institutional level is directed towards the national aim, namely pursuit of excellence in every field. This national goal is the common feature of the plans of lakhs of institutions in the country.

Co-operative in Nature

The institutional plan is the co-operative venture of the community, school management.

Reflects the State and the National Educational Policy

The institutional plan will reflect the educational policy at the state and the national levels. It will keep in view the broad guidelines issued by the State Education Department in the preparation of such plans.

Flexibility

This is a characteristic feature which differentiates the process of planing from below from the one of planning from above. The plans which have been prepared at the national and state levels for institutions have suffered from the element of rigidity.

Democratic Set-up

Institutional planning demands democratic producers within the school administration. Identification with the institutional plan on the part of the teacher is possible only in a democratic organization.

CONCLUSION

Just as a democratic administration is an important requisite for institutional planning, a fairly successful implementation will again result into furtherance to be democratic process with the school. Institutional plan is the set of policies and programmes prepared by an educational institution.

50

Western Political Thinkers

ROUSSEAU

INTRODUCTION

Rousseau was one of the great thinkers and educationists. His thought brought about the French revolution and this fact has been recognized even by Napoleon the Great.

Life Sketch: Rousseau was born of poor parents on 20th June, 1712. His father, he inherited studious temperament, but he also became careless. He did not stick to one job. First he worked in the office of the Registrar. Then he took up the job of a painter, but no place could attract him. Later on, he became a perfect vagabond.

Emile and Rousseau's thoughts about education: Emile contains Rousseau's thoughts about education. These thoughts are inspired by naturalism.

Works of Rousseau: Rousseau has talked about education in his various works. 'The New Heloise', 'Considerations on the Government of Poland', 'Social Contract', 'Political Economy', and contain his ideas about education is 'Emile' or 'Concerning Education'. It was publish in 1662 and contains revolutionary ideas. This book is like Plato's 'Republic' and contains ideas that have continued to influence the educationists upto date.

Rousseau's concept of Education – A Naturalist: Rousseau was a naturalist and so he was made nature or naturalism as the basis of education. He gave the slogans 'Back to Nature'. He has laid down that natural faculties of the children should be allowed to develop.

Source of education according to Rousseau: Rousseau has laid down 3 sources of education – Nature, Mind and Objects.

Various stages of education: Rousseau has divided the process of education into the following four stages and these stages have been Scientifically and Psychologically categorized.

Education for Infancy: According to Rousseau, this age ranges from birth to 5 years. According to Rousseau this is the stage of physical development so every attempt should be made to provide opportunity for physical development.

Education for Childhood: This period ranges from 5 years to 12 years. According to Rosseau, attempt should be made to brings about the development of the sense organs at this age of education.

Education for Boyhood: According to Rousseau this stage begins at 12 goes upto 15 years. This is the period of transition in the life of the child, and so education at this stage should be helpful in the 'development of his personality.' Education at this stage should contain labour, instructions and study.

Aims of Education: According to Rousseau, 'the process of education should facilitate the development of the child's innate powers and capacities. It should not confine the child to the acquisition of knowledge only'. He believed in imparting education through which the child may be able to live and survive. Economic efficiency has been covered in his aim of education.

Maxims or Traits of Rousseau's concept of Education: Rousseau's concept of education is based on the following maxims:

a. Child should be educated in the atmosphere of nature.
b. Child should be allowed to develop natural faculties. Teacher should have ideas about these faculties before he starts imparting education.
c. Education should be child centered.
d. It should bring about proper development of sense organs.
e. Education of a should be psychologically based.
f. Child should be left free to educate himself.
g. Education for women should aim at training the women to become ideal housewives.
h. The cardinal maxim of Rousseau's concept of education was that 'It is the development of the child's natural powers and abilities from within'.

Rousseau's concept of education and curriculum: We have already observed that Rousseau has divided education into four stages. The material of education for all these stages of education differs from one another.

a. **Curriculum for education for infancy:** At this stage of education, Rousseau has not laid down any set curriculum. He has suggested that the child be allowed to have full freedom to play.
b. **Curriculum of education for boyhood:** For this stage of education Rousseau has suggested the teaching of the followings – (i) Physical Sciences (ii) Language (iii) Mathematics (iv) Manual work (v) A trade (vi) Social Relations (vii) Music and (viii) Drawing.

For this stage of education, Rousseau has laid important on the development of judgment of power and reasoning and acquisition of habit of cleanliness, accuracy, precision and work.

d. Curriculum for education for Adolescence: For this stage of education, Rousseau has suggested the two following types of education:
   i. Moral Education
   ii. Religious Education

Apart from religious and moral education, the child at this stage should also be taught in the following: (a) History (b) Aesthetic education (c) Physical education (d) Sex education (e) Geography, etc.

JOHAUN FREDRICK HERBART

INTRODUCTION

Johaun Fredrick Herbart has been regarded as the father of educational psychology. He thinks that the child is the centre of all educational endeavors. The mind of the child is a unit and his development can take place only through psychology. Herbart has no faith in the existence of natural tendencies.

ACCORDING TO HERBARD

According to Herbard, soul is closely associated with the truth. And the body is a collection of truths. In so far as the soul is endowed with the power of presentation, it may be regarded as mind.

Soul is immortal. It remains alive even after the destruction of the body. Herbart does not believe in the freedom of will. Rather, he lays stress on concept of inner freedom which can grow in man when justice, equality and goodwill are in him.

HERBART OPINES

Herbart opines that it is possible to sum up education in one concept of morality. It includes perfection, equality, goodwill, internal freedom and justice. Education consists in the conquest of the lower impulses by the higher all together.

METHOD OF TEACHING

So far as the method is concerned, Herbart has said that the mind of the child works mainly in two stages, one is concentration and the other is reflection. Usually the child accepts ideas after being acquainted with them property. He then compares these ideas with the old ones. But, the ideas should be well co-ordinated so that it may be possible to use them properly. In this arena, one should know the formal steps suggested by Herbart which are: (a) presentation (b) generalization (c) application (d) preparation (e) association.

BASIC AIMS OF EDUCATION

Herbart is the view that the basic aims of education are the character-building and the development of versatile interests in the child. So, the curriculum should be (i) historical which includes literature, social science, history and language, and (ii) scientific which includes natural science, mathematics and geography. The method of teaching must be co-related.

IMPORTANCE OF DISCIPLINE

Herbart is fully aware of the importance of discipline in the educational system of the child. He believes that some sort of discipline is necessary for the character-building of the child. Discipline is good when it is capable of including in the child the spirit of self-respect, prestige and the anxiety to lead a well-organized life. Herbart says, "Pedagogy as a science is based on practical philosophy and on psychology".

COMMENT AND CONCLUSION

Herbart is the first educator who lays greater importance on the character building as the true aim of education. Herbart has connected instruction with character-training through interest and has provided techniques based on psychological considerations.

He makes the proper selection of the content of instruction and right method of presenting these selected contents incumbent on the teacher and contributing factors to the betterment of the goal which he has set for himself.

JOHN DEWEY

INTRODUCTION

John Dewey was a pragmatist which played a vital role in his conception of education. To him, education is the development of all those capacities in the individual which will enable him to control his environment and fulfil his faculties. John Dewey laid a greater importance on experiences which are socialized. He was against the prevalent system of education because it had no connection with practical life.

NO DEVELOPMENT WITHOUT EDUCATION

Dewey thought that there can be no progress without education. So education is absolutely essential for life. The school should be life and not a preparation for life. Education should be imparted to the children in such a way as to enable them to face the problems of real life.

According to Dewey, "Education as is traditionally conducted strikingly shows subordination of living present to a remote and precarious future. To prepare to get ready is the key-note." The process of education has two aspects – psychological and sociological. Of the two the psychological element is the basis of education. It is concerned with innate powers and instincts of the child. The study of education should be framed in accordance with the interest and natural tendencies of the pupil.

The sociological aspect is also very important. For, the aim of education should be to create an atmosphere by active participation in which the child may take part in the social awareness of the race. The knowledge of social awareness is for the proper modification of the powers and personalities of the children. The child develops his conduct, habits, character only by living within the society.

EDUCATION FOR CHILD

According to John Dewey, education should aim at the stimulation of the child's powers through the social medium. Its functions is to help growing of helpless young animal into a happy, moral and efficient human being. Education is important for living a social and happy life. The school should be planned in such a way as to help the pupils to realize some educative purposes. The chief function of the school will be to co-ordinate the diverse influences of the various social environments– family, workshop, religious organization into which the child enters.

EXPERIENCE IS THE BASIS OF EDUCATION

Education also controls and guides the inborn propensities of the child. But all these should be directed in socially desirable ways. Dewey thought experience as the basis of education. For it brings about the developments of human personality and mind. Education always reorganizes and reconstructs the human experience. Further, education has individual and social aims. The former enables a person to cultivate those principles which are of importance to him. The social aim includes (a) negative morality (b) economic efficiency and (c) positive morality.

LABORATORY SCHOOL

Dewey's conception of education was manifested in the form of an ideal school known as Laboratory School at Chicago. Here, school subjects were not prescribed. The programme of the Laboratory School was in the form of activities such as play, shop-work with tools and wood, cooking, sewing, weaving etc. Dewey considered the schools as a psychological and social necessity.

CURRICULUM SHOULD REFLECT THE SOCIAL LIFE

According to Dewey, curriculum should reflect the social life of the child and his social activities. It should not be rigid. The curriculum must be framed on the basis of the interest and tendencies of the child. Again the curriculum should follow the progressive organization of knowledge consisting of educative experiences and problems.

CHILD IS THE CENTRE OF EDUCATION

Dewey was of view that child is the prime of education. So, the method of teaching should be based on learning by doing, purpose and connection with the life of the child. The best method of teaching should have the following things, viz. (a) Data (b) Activity (c) Testing (d) Problem and (e) Hypothesis. It may be said that the ideas of Dewey in regard to the method of teaching are reflected Project Method.

EDUCATION – THE MIRROR OF THE DEMOCRATIC SET UP

According to Dewey, education is the mirror of the democratic way of life. He was in favour of democracy for teacher as well as for the pupil. The teacher must have a voice in the administration of the school which should be based on democratic policies. He also believed that a democratic system of education will develop the personality and capability of the child which are moral and self-directing.

CRITICISM

Several criticisms have been levelled against Dewey's conception of education. (a) The philosophy if education laid down by Dewey is not true. (b) Education has a purpose of its own. But Dewey did not believe it. (c) Dewey's views on education are not useful for women. (d) His philosophy of education is basically materialistic.

DEWEY'S EDUCATIONAL ROLE

We must not forget that Dewey has exerted a great influence in the filed of education. His educational contributions are:

a. Pragmatism in education.
b. Social efficiency as the basic aim of education.
c. Importance on the experiences of the child.
d. Sociology in education.
e. Close contract between society and school.
f. The doctrine of evolution applied to child-study.

In short, John Dewey has brought education more in accord with the actualities of present day life and placing the general policies that both philosophy and education should reflect main currents of contemporary thought.

FROEBEL

INTRODUCTION

Froebel was a great idealistic thinker and writer on education. He was influenced by the educational ideas of Kant and Hagel. According to Froebel, God is the sole source of all thinks. Things have come from the divine unity.

In all things there lives and reign have an eternal law - the Law of Unity. This eternal unity is God. It has three aspects — (a) Unity of origin - all things come from one source i.e., God. (b) Unity of substance — the spirit of soul animates both man and nature. (c) Unity of purpose — all things strive towards a divine perfection.

MAN'S LIFE IS A CONTINUOUS DEVELOPMENT

Froebel observed that man's life is a continuous progress. From his very birth, a child is anxious to do something. The teacher's contribution is like that of a gardener. He should create a proper environment for the development of the child. Froebel observed education to be a trait of creative self-development. Self-activity helps the child to realize his own nature.

AIM OF EDUCATION

To Froebel, the aim of education is to help the child in realizing unity in diversity and vice versa. It is through education that the innate tendencies of the child can be progressed. Froebel laid great effort on the importance of play in education. In other words, play is the foundation of his system of education. It is the purest, most spiritual activity of man.

KINDERGARTEN SYSTEM

Froebel was the founder of the "Kindergarten" system. It means the garden of the children. It is based on the principle of teaching children through play. According to Froebel, the school is a garden, and the teacher as a gardener helps the human plants to grow to beauty and perfection. The object of the 'Kindergarten System' is to give opportunity to the child for self-expression.

CONTRIBUTIONS

One of the greatest contributions of Froebel to the theory of education was his system of Kindergarten. He compared the children to tender plants whose nurture rests with the good and efficient teacher.

Froebel attached great importance to the school as an important social institutions where the children learn the essential things of life such as co-operation, mutual understanding and so on. His Kindergarten school was a miniature society where responsibility was shared by all, and also individual rights respected by all.

CONLCUSION

From the foregoing discussion we can conclude that, many of his (Froebel's) role have given a few phase to the education of the child and they shall continue to influence the society for a long time to come.

Froebel's idea of well-educated person was a balanced individual with well-developed abilities and well-adjusted social relationship and who would have, in addition, abundant spontaneity - a zest for tackling new problems, facing new situations, and mastering new knowledge.

DR. MARIA MONTESSORI

INTRODUCTION

Dr. Maria Montessori has exercised a lot of impact in the arena of education. Her greatest contribution to the modern education system is the natural tendencies of the child. In the present educational system, most of the educationists are very familiar with the Montessori system of education.

PRINCIPAL AIM

According to Montessori, the principal aim of education is to develop the physical and intellectual faculties of the child in a perfect manner. Her system of education is psychological in nature. To put in other words, she lays stress in the psychology of the child. She considers education as a process of betterment. The child is a body which grows and which develops from within. If any educational act is to be fractious, it will be only that which tends to help towards the complete unfolding of the individuality of the child. The development of the child is the same as the unfolding of hidden safflowers.

MONTESSORI SYSTEM OF SCHOOL

Montessori system of school is popularly known as "a children's house" where the atmosphere is suitable for the child to foster his individuality in the best possible manner. Many rooms and a garden are attached to this house. Children may play and take rest in the garden. The main room of the house is the place for the study of the children. The furniture and equipment of the children's house are specially made and designed for the use of children only.

THREE ESSENTIAL METHODS

Montessori system of teaching has three essential methods which are as follows:

a. Motor Education: It gives an opportunity of the child to work for himself. Only motor-education can bring about the physically developed personality of the child. The teacher should guide the children is a right manner so that they may work and handle things properly and also manage the house and the garden.
b. Sensory Education: It is completed through the didactic apparatus which consists of the following things – (i) three sets of solid insets (ii) pink cubes and brown prisms (iii) collection of various staffs (iv) two boxes, each contains sixty four coloured tablets (v) small wooden tables.
c. Language Teaching: It consists of a desk, small balls and cards with letters pasted on them. Letters are made of wood. Children move their hands over them. In this way, the child begins with reading and writing.

EFFECTS

The Montessori system of education has had a many sided effect on the work done in schools. It is a distinct step forward on Froebelian lines in the history of educational methods. Montessori has given a scientific approach to the child-education. Her system of education is based on the twin principles of democracy and individualism. Another vital contribution is that she lays great importance on the training of muscles as well as senses. Montessori shows a real feeling.

CONCLUSION

It is important that Montessori's concept of individuality is more biological than psychological. Her system of auto-education is mechanical and cannot solve the problems of actual life. There is no scope for self-expression. In her system, training of senses are formal. It is unsuitable for a gifted child.

JOHN LOCKE

INTRODUCTION

John Locke was born in England in the year 1632 in a conservative high family. His pre education began in Westminster School and then he joined Oxford University. He was appointed a teacher there having obtained the M.A. Degree. In this period, he met Lord Shaftsbury and began to look after his children. There was a great change in the thoughts of Locke by coming in contact with Lord Shaftsbury. He had great experience of his life is in Holland and France and he based his thoughts upon them.

EDUCATIONAL PHILOSOPHY

1. Locke thought that the old things should be discarded and he had great disgust for blind following and treading upon traditions.
2. Locke advised the elders to guide youngsters and the development of child should be under the shadow of the reasoning.
3. He had a broad outlook about development and wished that the ideals should get into the child upon the very foundation of childhood. He wanted to teach children the art of life by making them handsome, fit and socially developed.
4. He supported the utilitarian thoughts and had the nation. "It is not our duty to obtain full knowledge, on the other hand we should have that much knowledge which is necessary for our habits and actions".
5. He made the parents responsible for child education and declared that a child can be a progressed citizen only when he is kept in healthy and lovable environment.
6. Indicating the capacity of the children, he said that all the children cannot be taught in one and the same way. He wanted to keep children free with liberty.
7. Locke's advice on the bringing up of small children was that the children should be so brought up that they may possess good physique.

A CRITICAL EVALUATION

Locke's ideas gained very soon in France, England and Germany and the people began to give fresh valuation to education in the light of the those thoughts. Really Locke's thoughts are highly remarkable.

COMMENIUS

INTRODUCTION

Commenius held that education should be coloured with the religious thoughts, as the sole goal of the human being is to obtain salvation through the medium of God. He laid great emphasis upon the study of physics in education. He is remarkable to be the most valuable representative of the realistic movement and the greatest systematic builder in educational arena.

OBJECTIVES OF EDUCATION

Dr. Sitaram feels that the object of Commenius was to create piety and morality in an individual. He viewed, "The entire youth shall become learned in the science, pure in the morals, trained to piety and in this manner instructed in things necessary for the present and future life."

METHOD OF EDUCATION

He divided his method of education into four parts –

a. Mother Schools

b. Vernacular Schools

c. Latin Schools

d. The University

A DEFINITE CURRICULUM

Commenius gave a definite curriculum to all the four aforesaid schools and hoped that his curriculum will include all those subjects which are able to make a man wise, virtuous and pious.

WAYS OF EDUCATION

1. He believed that the knowledge obtained through perception is the real knowledge and so he advocated for scientific, perfect and natural education.
2. He revised that in the initial stages a child should be given oral education by "Look and Say Method".

EVALUATION

The thoughts of Commenius have been criticized by different writers but there is exaggeration that the philosophical insight and practical freedom of Commenius had great impact upon Rousseau and the other scholars.

Question Papers

RAJIV GANDHI UNIVERSITY

1999 (A)
B. A. I Year (Pass and Hons) Examination
PAPER-I
(Elements of Education)

Note: ***Answer Questions VI and VIII and four from the rest.***

I. How is the word 'Education' derived? 'Education is growth'. Briefly discuss the meaning of education as conveyed by the statement. 8+8

Or

What is the broader and narrower meaning of education?

II. What is the difference between formal and non-formal agencies of education? 8+8

III. What is educational sociology? Discuss its scope. 6+10

IV. School is a small community within a large community'. Explain the conditions under which the success and vitality of the school community depend. 16

V. Write short notes on any two of the following: 8+8

a. Education for leisure

b. Navodaya Vidyalaya

c. The role of Library as an agency of education

d. National Literacy Mission.

VI. Give an account of the salient features of the Vedic System of education. 16

VII. What do you mean by Introspection? Describe its advantages and limitations as a method of educational psychology. 6+10

Or

`Educational Psychology is a positive science and not a normative science.' Explain how far this statement is true. 16

VIII. Write brief notes on any two of the following: 10+10

a. The chief methods of instinct.

b. Characteristics of late childhood.

c. Emotional adjustment.

RAJIV GANDHI UNIVERSITY

2000 (A)
PAPER-I
(Elements of Education)

Note: *Answer Questions VI and VIII and four from the rest.*

I. What is 'Education'? What are the aims and functions? Discuss one of its aims of education. 2+4+4+6

Or

What do you mean by Non-formal Education? Discuss its utility in the present Indian context.

II. How would you define 'Modernization' in the education? What are the recent efforts in India to modernize the educational system? 8+8

Or

Write the names of philosophical schools of Vedic education. Do they bear relevance to the modern period?

III. What are Group Dynamics? What are the different patterns of group relationship among the students of a class? As a teacher, how would you help the isolated students? 4+4+8

Or

How Television and Cinema help in the education of a child? 8+8

IV. What do you mean by school and community? Suggest some possible ways and means of co-ordinating schools and community life through some educational programmes. 6+10

Or

Examine the role of education in international understanding. Suggest co-curricular activities at the college stage for promoting the sense of international understanding. 8+8

V. Write short notes on (any two) : 8×2

a. New Policy on Education-1986

b. National Integration

c. Education for all

d. Human Resource Development.

VI. Explain how the study of Educational Psychology helps a teacher in performing his duties and responsibilities. 8+8

Or

Discuss the nature and scope of Educational Psychology.

VII. Discuss the factors in influencing development during childhood and adolescence.

Or

What is Sociology? Write the contributions of Sociology to the educational theory.

VIII. Write short notes on the following (any two) : 10x2

a. Interest

b. Aims of Education

c. Methods of Modification of Instinct.

d. Methods of Studying Children's Emotion.

RAJIV GANDHI UNIVERSITY

2001 (A)
PAPER-I
(Elements of Education)

(Maximum Marks 90 for Regular Candidates)
(Maximum Marks 100 for Private Candidates)

Note: ***(i) All candidates are to answer any five questions.***
(Questions I to IX). Question X is compulsory for Private Candidates)

I. Explain the concept of education. Why is education regarded as a lifelong process ? 9+9

II. What are the different aims of education? Which of them do you like the best? Give reasons for your choice. 5+5+8

III. What do you mean by agencies of education? How family and television help in the education of a child? 9+9

IV. What is 10+2+3 pattern of education? Explain the principles underlying this pattern of education. Discuss the different problems for implementing the same. 5+5+8

V. Write short notes on any two of the following: 9+9

a. Gurukul systems of education.
b. Role of Mass media.
c. Open University.
d. International Understanding.

VI. Define Instincts. Explain the characteristics of Instincts. Describe the different methods of modifying Instincts. 5+5+8

VII. Discuss the relationship between Sociology and Education. How does Sociology affect educational thought and practice? 9+9

VIII. What are the different methods of Educational Psychology? Discuss any one method by stating its merits and demerits. 6+12

IX. What do you mean by Adolescence? Explain the basic features and problems of Adolescents. 5+13

(For Private Candidates only)

X. Write short notes on any two of the following: 5+5

a. Relationship between School and Society.
b. Group Behaviour.
c. Role of Education for Modernization.
d. Methods of Children's Emotions.

RAJIV GANDHI UNIVERSITY

2002 (A)
PAPER-I
(Elements of Education)

(Maximum Marks 90 for Regular Candidates)
(Maximum Marks 100 for Private Candidates)

Note: ***(i) All candidates are to answer any five questions.***
(Questions I to IX). Question X is compulsory for Private Candidates)

I. What do you understand by the term Education? Discuss fully with suitable examples. 18

II. What should be the aims of education in present day India? How far have they been realized in actual practice? 14+4

III. Describe the role of school and family as agencies of education. 9+9

IV. Discuss the nature and scope of Educational Psychology. 9+9

V. Describe the important characteristics of Infancy and Adolescence period. 9+9

VI. What is Emotion? Explain its characteristics. Can Emotions be modified? Explain with suitable examples. 5+5+8

VII. What is Educational Sociology? Explain the different social factors affecting Education. 8+10

VIII. What are the important features of Ancient Education? Can you point your any specific aspects which can be relevant in the present society? 10+8

(For Private and Late College candidates only)

IX. Write a note on any one :

a. Group Behaviour.

b. Introspection Method.

c. Buddhist Education.

RAJIV GANDHI UNIVERSITY

2003 (A)

B.A. 1st Year (Pass and Hons.) Examination

PAPER - I (Old Course)

(Elements of Education)

Note: *(i) Answer question X and any four from the rest.*

I. Define Education. Why is education regarded as a lifelong process? 20

II. What do you understand by Individual and Social aims of Education? How far is it possible to strike a balance between them? Discuss. 20

III. Discuss the role of Family and Television is agencies of education. 20

IV. What is Educational Psychology? Why should be study of Psychology be essential to a teacher? Explain. 20

V. Define Human growth and development. Write down the important characteristics of Childhood? 20

VI. What do you by Instinct? How can Instincts be utilized for educational purpose? 20

VII. Define Educational Sociology. Discuss the relationship between Education and Sociology. 20

VIII. Discuss the chief characteristics of Post-Vedic education. Point out its different aspects which can be relevant in the present system of education. 20

IX. Define National Integration. Discuss different obstacles in the way of National Integration. How can these obstacles be removed. 20

X. The Private/Late College candidates will write short notes on any two and the Regular candidates any one of the following: 10x2=20

10x1=20

a. Social factors affecting Education.

b. Experimental Method.

c. Education for Modernization.

d. 10+2+3 Pattern of Education.

e. Functions of Emotion in human life.

RAJIV GANDHI UNIVERSITY

2003 (A)

B.A. PAPER-I (New Course - Pass and Hons.)

Note : (i) All candidates are to attempt any five questions out of I to IX.

Question X is compulsory for Private/Late College candidates only.

I. Clarify the meaning of Education. Should education be regarded as a process or achievement? Give arguments for your answer. 10+4+3

II. What are the different Aims of Education? Which particular aim would you especially emphasize in the context of individual and social welfare? 8+10

III. What do you mean by "Educational Ladder"? Describe the ladder of education suggested by Secondary Education Commission (1952-53) and its important features of each level. 6+6+6

IV. Define Educational Psychology. Discuss the nature and scope of Educational Psychology. 10+8

V. What is Adolescence? Give the Physical and Emotional characteristics of this period. 8+10

VI. What do you mean by Instincts? Describe McDougal's classification of Instincts. 8+10

VII. What is Educational Sociology? Discuss critically the social factors, which affect educational system of a society. 8+10

VIII. Write notes on any two of the following: 18

a. International Understanding.

b. Modernization and Education.

c. The James Lange Theory of Emotion.

(For Private and Late College candidates only)

IX. Write a note on any of the following: 10

a. Utility of Education Technology in formal and non-formal education.

b. Recommendation of Education Commission (1964-66) on educational ladder.

c. New Education Policy on the structure of education.

RAJIV GANDHI UNIVERSITY

2005 (A)

B.A. 1st Year (Pass and Hons.) Examination

PAPER - I (New Course)

(Elements of Education)

Maximum Marks	:	*100 (for Private/Late College)*
	:	*90 (for Regular)*
Pass Marks	:	*33% (for Pass)*
	:	*35% (for Hons)*
Time	:	*Three Hours.*

Note : *i.* ***Answer any five questions from Question Nos. I to IX.***
ii. ***Question No. X is only for Private / Late College candidates.***
iii. ***The figures in the margin indicate full marks for the questions.***

I. Define 'Education'. Distinguish between formal and non-formal education. 10+8

II. What are the different Aims of Education? Discuss in detail any three of them. 6+12

III. What is 1+2+3 Pattern of Education? Explain the principles underlying this pattern of education ? 10+8

IV. Explain the concept of Learning. Illustrate the laws of learning and give detail of any one of them. 8+10

V. What is Human Development? Discuss the topic of heredity and environment for human development. 8+10

VI. What is Instinct? Distinguish between Instinct and Emotions. Suggest ways and means for the emotional training of the school children. 6+6+6

VII. What is Educational Technology? Explain the nature and scope of educational technology. 10+8

VIII. Write short notes on any two of the following:

a. Moral and Cultural aims of education.

b. Adolescence.

c. Hardware and Software.

d. International understanding.

IX. 'Education has been one of the most influenced instruments of modernization' Discuss.

(For Private/Late College Candidates only)

X. Write short not on any one of the following:

a. Kothari Commission

b. Factors of Socialization

c. National Integration.

RAJIV GANDHI UNIVERSITY

2007 (A)
DISTANCE EDUCATION
B.A. I Year Examination
EDUCATION
Paper – I
(Elements of Education)

Time	:	*Three Hours*
Maximum Marks	:	*70*
Pass Marks	:	*33%*

Note : *i.* ***Answer any five questions.***
ii. ***The figures in the margin indicate full marks for the questions.***

I. What do you mean by 'Education'? Discuss briefly the formal and non-formal type of education with examples. 6+8

II. Describe the individual and Social Aims of Educational. How will you synthesize them? 10+4

III. What is 'Educational Ladder'? In context of this, state the recommendations of Secondary Education Commission (SEC) 1952-53. 4+10

IV. Define 'Learning'. Explain briefly the various laws of learning with their classroom implications. 4+10

V. Differentiate between Growth and Development. Discuss the principles of development with appropriate examples. 6+8

VI. What are Emotions? Describe the characteristics and Educational implications of Emotions. 6+8

VII. What is meant by 'Educational Technology'? Enumerate the Hardware and Software approaches of Educational Technology in detail. 6+8

VIII. Define 'Educational Sociology'. Discuss its nature and scope. 4+4+6

IX. What is 'Social Change'? Explain the role of education for social change. 6+8

X. Write short notes on any two of the following: 7×2=14

a. Narrower and broader meaning of Education.

b. Cultural Aims of Education.

c. Central Theory of Emotions.

d. International Understanding and role of Education in it.

RAJIV GANDHI UNIVERSITY

2008 (A)
B.A. 1st Year (Pass and Hons.) Examination
EDUCATION
PAPER - I (Old and New Course)
(Elements of Education)

Maximum Marks : *100 (for Private/Late College)*
: *90 (for Regular)*
Pass Marks : *33% (for Pass)*
: *35% (for Hons)*
Time : *Three Hours.*

Note : *i.* ***Answer any five questions from Question Nos. I to IX (for all candidates).***
ii. ***Question No. X is only for Private / Late College candidates.***
iii. ***The figures in the margin indicate full marks for the questions.***

I. What is Education? Illustrate the nature and scope of Education. 6+12

II. Explain aims of Education with examples. 18

III. What is New Pattern of Education? Discuss New Education Policy on the structure of Education. 6+12

IV. Explain the concept of Learning. Illustrate the laws of Learning with example. 6+12

V. What do you mean by Growth and Development? Elaborate the main features of Growth and Development at adolescence stage. 6+12

VI. What do you mean by Instinct? Explain McDougal's concept of Instinct. Discuss its educational implications. 6+6+6

VII. What is Educational Technology? Discuss various types of Educational Technology. 6+12

VIII. Define Educational Sociology. Explain the role of the Education in Social Development. 6+12

IX. Write Notes on any two of the following:
a. Modernization and Education
b. National Integration
c. Heredity and Environment
d. Types of Education

(For Private and Late College candidates only)

X. Write short note on any one of the following: 10
a) Nature and scope at Educational Sociology
b) Utility of Educational Technology
c) Socialization

RAJIV GANDHI UNIVERSITY

2008 (A)
DISTANCE EDUCATION
B.A. I Year Examination
EDUCATION
Paper – I
(Elements of Education)

Time	:	*Three Hours*
Maximum Marks	:	*70*
Pass Marks	:	*33%*

Note : *i)* ***Answer any five questions.***
ii) ***The figures in the margin indicate full marks for the questions.***

I. Discuss the concept of Education. Differentiate between Formal and Non-formal Education. 6+8

II. Discuss the major aims of Education. 14

III. What is 10+2+3 Pattern of Education? Discuss the advantages of implementing. 6+8

IV. Explain the meaning, nature and scope of Educational Psychology. 4+5+5

V. Differentiate between Growth and Development. Discuss the principles of Growth and Development. 7+7

VI. Explain the meaning and characteristics of Instinct. Describe the different methods of modifying Instinct. 6+8

VII. Discuss the meaning nature and scope of Educational Technology. 4+5+5

VIII. What do you mean by Socialization? Discuss the agencies of Socialization. 4+10

IX. Define 'Social Change'. Explain the various factors influencing social change. 6+8

X. Write notes on any two of the following: 7×2

a. National Integration.
b. Laws of Learning.
c. Characteristics of Adolescence Period.
d. Democratic Aims of Education.

DIBRUGARH UNIVERSITY

Education - 2007 (Major)
B.A. First Paper
(Philosophical and Sociological Foundation of Education)

Candidates eligible for Internal Assessment shall answer Question Nos. 1 to 7 *Full Marks - 90*

Candidates not eligible for Internal Assessment are to answer Question Nos. 1 to 8. *Full Marks - 100*

1. Complete the following sentences : 1x10=10
   i. Negative education was introduced by ______________.
   ii. 'Democracy and Education' was written by ______________.
   iii. The word education is derived from two Latin words 'educare' and ______________.
   iv. The IGNOU was established in the year ______________.
   v. The word 'Society' is derived from the Latin word ______________.
   vi. Education is the natural, harmonious and progressive development of man's ______________.
   vii. Education is the dynamic side of ______________.
   viii. The socializing process through which an individual places oneself in the position of another person feels that same may be known as ______________.
   ix. The three language formula was first introduced by ______________.
   x. Curriculum is derived from the Latin word ______________.
2. Write short notes on the followings : 4x5 = 20
   a. Vocational aim of education.
   b. Community centered curriculum.
   c. Educational sociology.
   d. Vedic education.
   e. The role of family in the Socialization Process.
3. Define aims of Education. What are the determinants of aims of education? Explain each of them. 2+8

   Or

   Explain Individual and Social Education and its relationship to each other. 5+5
4. Make a comparison of Naturalism, Idealism and Pragmatism with respect to. 6+6+6
   a. Aims of Education.
   b. Method of Teaching and
   c. Position of Teacher.

Or

Describe how Vedanta, Gita and Buddhist Philosophy influence the education system of India.

5. Write a note on different view points regarding the nature of curriculum.

Or

Make a list of Co-curricular activities in relation to different aspects.

6. Describe the various aspects of Education for the economic prosperity of our country.

Or

What is Social Change? Discuss the importance of Education as an instrument of Social Change. 3+10

7. What is meant by the term Social Mobility ? What are the causes and factors of Social Mobility ? 2+8

Or

Elucidate the relationship between Education and Social Mobility and discuss how Education affects Social Mobility. 5+5

In lieu of internal assessment

8. Describe the differences between Sociology and Educational Sociology. 10

Or

Write briefly on Democracy and Education.

DIBRUGARH UNIVERSITY

Education - 2008 (Major)

B.A. First Paper

(Philosophical and Sociological Foundation of Education)

Full Marks - 90

1. Choose the correct one: 1×5=5

a. Education in broader term means.

i. Acquisition of knowledge
ii. Training of individual
iii. Acquisition of some skills
iv. Harmonious development of individual

b. Which of the following is the contribution of Rousseau to education?

i. Education for freedom
ii. Education for democracy
iii. Education for state control
iv. Education for Nationalism

c. Aims of education are determined by human being for the good of the

i. Individual
ii. Society
iii. Individual and society both
iv. Neither the individual nor the society

d. A characteristic of secondary social group is

i. Inclusive relationship
ii. Personal relationship
iii. Spontaneity of relationship
iv. Emphasis on interest and competition

e. Leadership in social change may be provided by

i. Education
ii. Political change
iii. Economic reforms
iv. Social reforms

2. Fill up the blanks : 1x5=5

a. Educational behaviour is derived from ______________ of education.

b. Development of a nation in the main aim of ______________ education.

c. John Dewey was one of the chief exponents of ______________.

d. Democracy is not only a political philosophy but also a ______________ philosophy.

e. ______________ is the instrument of social change.

3. Write short notes on the following : 4x5
   a. Education and development of human values.
   b. Relationship between education and philosophy.
   c. Co-curriculur activities and their importance.
   d. Importance of education in a democracy.
   e. Role of education to meet the demands of a new social order.
4. a. Define the term 'Education'. How can education help in the proper utilization of human as a resource towards development? 2+10

   Or

   b. Define the term 'Education'. How does education function as a means towards individual development? 2+10
5. Explain the main features of naturalism as a school of philosophy and its contribution towards present-day curriculum. 6+6
6. a. Explain at least four different aims of education, keeping in view the needs of 21st century. 3x4

   Or

   b. i. Discuss the importance of discipline in the present social life. 6
   ii. Explain the role of the Teacher and Pupil in establishing discipline in the social life. 3+3
7. a. What is meant by the term 'Education Sociology'? Discuss its aims. 3+3
   b. How can Education promote Culture? 6
8. Define the term 'Socialization'. Discuss the role of education as an instrument of social change. 3+9

(In Lieu of Internal Assessment)

10. "Education is a continuous lifelong social process." Explain. 10

DIBRUGARH UNIVERSITY

Education
2007 (July)
B.Ed. First Paper
Education in Emerging India

Full Marks : 90
Pass Marks : 36
Time : 4 hours

The figures in the margin indicate full marks for the questions:

1. a. Define Culture. Describe briefly the common components of Indian cultural heritage. 2+8

Or

Give a brief account of the central teachings of Vedanta Philosophy with their educational significance. 10

What is 'Naturalism in Education'? Explain briefly the principles underlying naturalistic education. 2 + 8

Or

What is ' Negative Education' of Rousseau ? Discuss the chief characteristics of Negative Education with their educational implications. 3 + 7

2. Describe the following precisely: 5 × 3
   a. Education as a Product
   b. Education as Growth
   c. Education as profession

Or

What is Modernization? What are its attributes? How can education help in the process of modernization? 4 + 5 + 6

3. What is 'Social Stratification'? Mention the major causes of inequality in educational opportunity in India. 3+7

Or

Describe objectively how education can play the role for economic development in the State. 10

4. Enumerate the important features of the Brahmanic System of education in ancient India. Point out those features which are still relevant. 10+5

Or

What are the major recommendations of the Wood's Despatch, 1854 ? Analyze them critically. 9 + 6

5. Bring out the significant developments in the educational field during 1986-2006 in India. 15

6. What is meant by 'Environmental Degradation'? How does it affect quality of life? How can environmental education promote quality of life? 4 + 5 + 6

Or

What is Privatization? Discuss the recent trend of privatization of education in India. Is it desirable? 3+8+4

DIBRUGARH UNIVERSITY

2008

B.Ed. First Paper

(Education in Emerging India)

Time : 4 hours

Pass Marks : 36

1. Describe the components of our Cultural heritage. Write the four characteristics of our common cultural heritage with necessary illustrations. 6+4

   Or

   Define Samkhya Philosophy. Explain how Samkhya Philosophy influenced upon aims and curriculum of Modern Indian Education. 2+3+5
2. Compare the impact of Idealism and Naturalism on education with special reference to its aims, methodology curriculum and role of teacher. 10
3. a. Discuss the meaning and scope of Education. 5

   Or

   Explain the role of education as an agency of Human Resource Development

   b. Write a note on how Education can accelerate the process of Modernization. 10
4. Highlight the contribution of education in promoting equality of educational opportunities. 10

   Or

   Explain the role of education as a tool Economic Development and Economic Growth in India. 5+5
5. Describe the salient features of Vedic System of education. What aspects of Vedic System of Education are relevant even today? 10+5

   Or

   Write why Lord Macaulay was appointed to review the Education problems in India. Critically analyze his recommendations. 5+10
6. Describe the significant developments in the field of Education during the period 1966-1986. 15
7. Write a brief note on any three of the following: 5x3

   a. Population Education, with special reference to its aims and content area.

   b. Value Education in Indian context with special reference to its objective and inculcation strategies.

   c. Sarva Shiksha Abhiyan and its progress in Assam.

   d. Privatization of Education, its merits and demerits.

GAUHATI UNIVERSITY

2008

B.Ed. First Paper

Philosophical and Sociological Foundations of Education

Full Marks : 100

The figures in the margin indicate full marks for the questions.

Answer any five questions.

1. What do you mean by aims of Education? Discuss the Sociocultural, Political and economic factors influencing Education Aims. 5+15
2. What is "Naturalism"? Rousseau has been classified as one of the greatest advocates of Naturalism, but his Philosophic position was essentially idealistic. Discuss the statement. 5+15
3. Elucidate the concept "Educational Reconstruction". Discuss the Educational constructions of Mahatma Gandhi towards Educational reconstruction. 5+15
4. What do you mean by "Environment"? State the causes responsible for environmental pollution. Suggest measures for environmental protection and pollution control. 4+8+8
5. What do you understand by the term "Professional Ethics"? Discuss the Professional Ethics to be followed by a teacher in relation to students, colleagues and parents. 5+15
6. Discuss the interdependence of school and Community. Explain the ways and means of co-ordinating school community functions. 10+10
7. Write notes on any two: 10x2
   i. Constitutional Rights and obligations of citizens.
   ii. National Policy of Education, 1986.
   iii. Population and Quality of life.
   iv. Education for Peace.
   v. Traditions and Modernity.

RAJIV GANDHI UNIVERSITY

December – 2008
B. Ed. (First Semester) Examination
EDUCATION
Paper : B.Ed. - 401
(Teacher and Society)

Time : 3 Hours
Maximum Marks : 80
Pass Marks : 35%

Note : i. Answer all questions.
ii. The figures in the margin indicate full marks for the question.

I. Explain the meaning of 'Purusartha' and 'Nishkama Karma' with their bearing on value education. 8+8

Or

Discuss the meaning, nature and scope of Education. 16

II. Discuss the educational thoughts of M.K. Gandhi. 16

Or

Discuss the contribution of John Dewey to Educational Thought and Practices. 16

III. How can education inculcate Principles of Equality and Secularism among the Children? Discuss in the light of educational provisions relating to these aspects. 8+8

Or

Deliberate on education for Human Rights and Education as Fundamental Right in the context of Indian Society. 8+8

IV. Discuss the meaning and factors of Social Change. 16

Or

Elaborate the meaning of National and Emotional Integration. Discuss the role of Education in promoting National Integration. 6+10

V. Write notes on any two of the following: 8×2=16

a. Status of Teaching Profession.
b. Teacher as a Leader in the class and community.
c. Role of NCTE for quality Teacher Education.
d. Swami Vivekananda's thoughts on Education.
e. Aims of education according to Idealism.

Select Bibliography

Brameld, Theodore, Patterns of Educational Philosophy. A democratic Interpretation (World Book Company, Tarrytown-on-Hudson, New York, 1950)

.........................., Philosophies of Education in Cultural Perspective (The Dryden Press, Inc., New York, 1955)

Bremeld, Theodor, Toward a Reconstructed Philosophy of Education (The Dryden Press, Inc., New York, 1956)

Broudy, Harry et al., Philosophy of Education (University of Illinois Press, Urbana, II, 1967)

Brown, L. M., General Philosophy in Education (McGraw-Hill Book Company, New York, 1966)

Brown, F. J., Educational Sociology (Prentice Hall, Inc., 1961)

Chaube, S. P., Foundations and Guidelines of Modern Education, Ram Prasad & Sons, 1957, Agra.

.........................., Recent Philosophies of Education in India, Ram Prasad & Sons, 1967, Agra.

Chaube, S. R., Shiksha Ke Samajashastriya Adhar, Vinod Pustak Mandir, Agra, 1976.

Childs, John L., Pragmatism and American Education (Holt, Rinehart and Winston, Inc., New York, 1956).

Das Gupta, S. N., Study of Patanjali.

Datta, D. M., The Six Ways of Knowing, Calcutta University, 1960.

Dupuls, Adrian and Norberg Robert, Philosophy and Education (The Bruce Publishing Company, Mijwaupee, 1964)

Gruber, Fredrick C., Foundations for a Philosophy of Education (Thomas Y. Crowell Company, New York, 1961).

Hardie, O. D., Truth and Fallacy in Educational Theory, 1942, Macmillan.

Kilpatric, William, H., Education for a Changing Civilization. (The MacMillan Company, 1926).

Lodge, Rapert C., Philosophy of Education (Harper and Row, Publishers, Incorporated, New York, 1947).

Mac Donald, John, A Philosophy of Education (Scott Foreman and Company, Chicago, 1967).

Pandey, R. S., Shiksha Darshan Ka Sarveshan, Central Book Depot, Allahabad, 1981.

Pathak, Guptajit, A Systematical Approach To Elements of Education, G and Pathak Prakashan Parishad, Bezera, Kamrup, Assam, 2009.

Phemix, Phillip H., Philosophy of Education (Holt, Rinehart and Winston, In., New York, 1958).

Prankena, William, K, Three Historical Philosophies of Education (Scott Foresman and Company, Chicago, 1965).

Reid, Lonis, A., Philosophy and Education (William Heinemann, London, 1962).

Russel, B., Philosophy, 1927, Norton.

Sampurnananda, Yoga Darshan, Hindi Samiti, Lucknow, 1965.

Scheffler, Jorael (Ed.), Philosophy and Education : Modern Readings (Allyn and Bacon, Inc. Boston, 1958).

Ulich, Robert, Fundamentals of Democratic Education, 1940, American Book.

Ward, Leo, Philosophy of Education (Henry Regnery Company, Chicago, 1966).

Washburn, C. W., Living Philosophies of Education, 1940, Day.

Weber, Christian O., Basic Philosophies of Education (Holt, Rinehart and Winston, Inc., New York, 1960).